LOST IN TRANSITION

**HOW BUSINESS LEADERS CAN SUCCESSFULLY
TAKE CHARGE IN NEW ROLES**

Richard Elsner & Bridget Farrands

CYAN

 Marshall Cavendish
Business

First published in 2006 by:

Marshall Cavendish Limited
119 Wardour Street
London W1F 0UW
United Kingdom
T: +44 (0)20 7565 6000
F: +44 (0)20 7734 6221
E: sales@marshallcavendish.co.uk
www.marshallcavendish.co.uk

and

Cyan Communications Limited
119 Wardour Street
London W1F 0UW
United Kingdom
T: +44 (0)20 7565 6120
E: sales@cyanbooks.com
www.cyanbooks.com

A CIP record for this book is available from the British Library

ISBN-13 978-904879-87-9
ISBN-10 1-904879-87-X

Designed by Grade Design Consultants, London
www.gradedesign.com

Printed and bound in Great Britain by TJ International Ltd, Padstow, Cornwall

Contents

Introduction:
The great unspoken struggle

New jobs should come clearly labelled with a health warning: this job could seriously change how you are and how you act in your organisation. Taking charge in a new role – the time we refer to as transitions – is to enter a time filled with personal potential. It can promise you the greatest of discoveries about yourself at the same time as creating opportunities to make a memorable difference to your place of work. Most people, as they start on their first day, look ahead with exactly this kind of hope and aspiration for themselves. Some might still be enjoying the celebrations of getting the job, basking in the spotlight of their success. And the first few days do little to dent the optimism and positive anticipation of arriving in a new role.

But it seems that, to realise any of these hopes for personal and organisational potential, means also being ready for some unexpected surprises and losses. You may be surprised to feel confused and indecisive just at the very time you want to appear clear and decisive; you may feel overwhelmed and anxious just at the very time you want to be known as composed and dynamic. As to delivering your goals: they may be contradictory and ambiguous, when you had thought you knew exactly what you were brought here to achieve. You are surprised to find that the organisation you are joining is hard to fit into the description you had been given of it and your confidence seems to dive most mornings when you walk through the door. Nobody tells you any of this beforehand and it's likely you won't be expecting these reactions or experiences. And – just maybe – your transition into a new role won't match any part of this description. Maybe ...

As authors of this book, we have had the privilege, through our research and consulting work, to look behind the veil usually put over taking on a new job. With the help of many teams and leaders we have lifted that veil to see what really goes on. What gets lost in transitions? How are such losses valuable? Does it have to be like this? Is it possible to lose confidence, self-esteem, your way and still end up successful? Can transitions be a time of gain also? We believe that there is an untold story about what really happens to leaders, teams and to their organisations in the vital phase of a new leader arriving: the phase of transition. Here is that story.

* * *

Lost in Transition is a story filled with drama, tension, anguish and suffering. It is also a story full of triumph, delight, achievement and joy. They are one and the same story and it's one of the best-kept secrets in the world of work: what really goes on for people who change jobs, especially senior jobs? What is the *personal* experience of this time – roughly the first six to nine months and how do people handle themselves through considerable change and adaptation to a new working world? What do new leaders need to pay attention to in the organisational world around them as they step into their new role? Little is known and even less is said about this period, yet for many leaders it is a time of struggle, chaos and search for mastery and personal coherence. We discovered that, in time and if well handled, transitions are opportunities too for step changes in self-understanding and transformation, but only after grappling with personal demons and the fearless confronting of their own and others' outdated limitations.

What really happens?

We were deeply curious too about what went on in an organisation when a new leader joined. If senior, they inevitably always disturb the status quo, so how was that handled by the leader, his team, his boss and colleagues? How do new leaders, without much understanding of the context, make choices and decisions about what to tackle? What role does their boss have in making sure they join successfully? And these questions then got us interested in how the usually unspoken personal experiences of transition got mixed up with the leader's organisational remit. We had seen many situations in our consulting and business experience where new arrivals had seemed to act without enough regard for the organisation's history, or apparently without respect for what was precious and carefully guarded about the identity of the organisation. This took us into asking whether there might be ways for new leaders to understand such tensions without being disabled from bringing about the change that most are charged with today. And when and if they did feel disabled, how did their personal frame of reference about themselves at this time affect their actions?

The research that debunks the myths

As we got more interested in what happens to organisations and their leaders when each meets the other, we began to realise that our own knowledge was limited. We were as prone to the vague statements and holding only general surface understanding about this situation, much like everyone else. It was only when we each got involved in direct and deeper exploration of the topic that we began to appreciate what really goes on for new leaders and their organisations when each finds the other. *Lost in Transition* is the result of two in-depth research studies as well as ongoing research and work with leaders taking on new roles, into what makes for successful job change.

Research study 1 The personal experience of transition: What doesn't get talked about

In 2002, Bridget Farrands found herself working with several senior leaders who, coincidentally, had all recently started new roles. Her agenda was a varied and broad one, ranging from a request to help the leader hit the ground running to providing specific advice on how to lead culture change. After several meetings over a few weeks she began to notice some similar issues emerging from her contact with these leaders. They owned up to feelings of low confidence, of disorientation at the scale and scope of the brief they had to fulfil. They complained of bosses who were uninterested in them and unavailable to exchange views on emerging issues; they spoke about the stress and effort involved in looking like they knew what they were about. Some wondered how they would decide when and if to change team members; others grappled with the domestic pressures of house and school moves and the dislocation to their partner's lives.

As these experiences became the main topic of discussion at meetings, Bridget started to look for more information to enable her to better support her clients. And found none. Or at least none that dealt directly with this internal personal struggle. So she set about finding out more herself. Over the next 14 months she interviewed nearly 50 leaders from a range of industries – manufacturing, retailing, FMCG, advertising and the public sector – about their experience of moving into a new role. She recorded and transcribed their interviews and used them to identify themes these experiences had in common – regardless of sector, role or specific level. What she found were some surprising discoveries about how leaders themselves accounted for successful transitions.

Three issues stood out through all the interviews:

1 The importance of keeping these experiences **secret** from everyone around the leader in the organisation. The need to protect the leader's image of invincibility and unruffled coping was strongly held and any challenge to this way of looking at their situation was usually resisted. We discovered, as we began to apply our research work to transitioning leaders, that this secret keeping was itself part of what slowed down the success of the transition.

2 The **undiscussability** of the experience: the topic itself was out of bounds, as though by talking about low self-confidence or the need for personal change these would somehow incapacitate the leader further. The philosopher, Ludwig Wittgenstein, believed that we cannot think about something if we cannot speak about it. We couldn't agree more. We have never advocated a no-holds barred Oprah Winfrey–style of self-disclosure. But we do know that it's hard to manage what can't be discussed.

3 How **unprepared** leaders had been for the work of transition itself. Some held only general models of how they would experience this change and what to do about it; for others entering and understanding the new role and organisation were secondary to making their mark and establishing their positions. Few could see that transitions are a process and range of experiences that need managing as much as any of their business tasks and objectives. Using this experience as a rich seam of potential for personal change also passed unnoticed, although several leaders described how some of their tougher past experiences had shaped their present practice as leaders.

Where's the boss in all this?

Only a handful of leaders spoke about the positive role their boss had played in supporting them into their new role: more common was to find that their boss was not even present on their first day. In the early stage of arriving in the role, demanding bosses generated very reactive responses, scurrying around to "please" and reassuring them that the new leader was on the case. As the transition progressed and confidence increased, leaders dug their heels in and refused to collude with the unhelpful behaviours of the boss.

For most leaders there was a direct correlation between the relationship with the boss and their own confidence to act. It's hardly a surprise to hear that the boss has such a pivotal role in ensuring the successful arrival of the leader, so why is it so unusual for new leaders to get the right level of direction and sponsorship from their boss?

The commonest source of support and sounding boards leaders spoke about were friends or colleagues from outside their current organisation. In the section 2 on the reality of transition, we describe the territory of transitions in more detail and what leaders found had

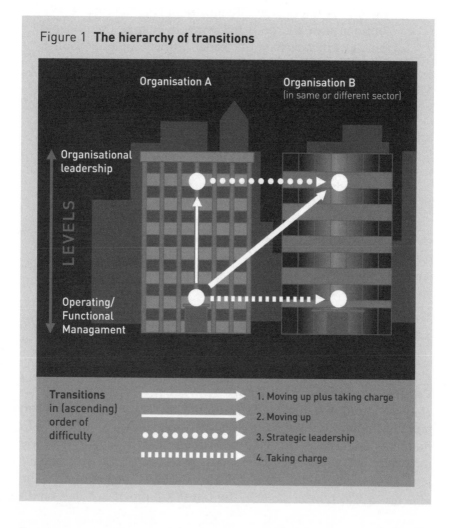

Figure 1 **The hierarchy of transitions**

Organisation A

Organisation B
(in same or different sector)

Organisational leadership

LEVELS

Operating/
Functional
Managament

Transitions
in (ascending)
order of
difficulty

1. Moving up plus taking charge

2. Moving up

3. Strategic leadership

4. Taking charge

worked to make different aspects of their transition a success, including how they managed their boss.

Leaping across, up and over

Some transitions are more complex and tougher than others. The (significant) challenges of any transition are heightened because of the larger thresholds that the leader has to simultaneously cross and manage. The more there are of these, the greater are the risks and pressures the leader will have to face; and these in turn impact the time it will take the leader to prove his worth to the rest of the organisation.

The significant thresholds the leader has to cross are:

- Entering a new sector or industry.
- Moving from one organisation to another but within the same sector.
- Moving up to a larger functional role from within a function but where the specialism has to involve a wider remit.
- Moving into a senior general management role where the leader's specialism is less vital to the content of the role.

Research study 2 **The organisational forces which impact transitions: What goes on around the leader**

Now to our second research study. In 1999, Richard Elsner and three other consultants (George Binney, Gerhard Wilke and Colin Williams) started to research what actually happens during the phase of transition. All four were intrigued to understand why so many of their leader clients were struggling to achieve what was expected of them and were apparently not enjoying their leadership role (as much as we thought they should!). Ashridge Management College in the UK and HEC/CPA business school in France financed the study and contributed considerable brain power. The research team expanded to ten, including Professor Gilles Amado from HEC/CPA. In a first round of interviews with leaders and HR professionals in 30 corporations and government departments, the team uncovered two facts that startled it. First, in almost all of the organisations canvassed, the people interviewed said that the current and increasing rate of disappointing performance by new leaders was a major source of concern and, what is more, of perplexity to them. Second, in none of the organisations canvassed were new leaders apparently given any support to anticipate and then cope with the difficulties which taking on a new leadership role entailed.

The team wondered might the second fact be one cause of the first? Through observation of what happened to new leaders as they took charge, could one nail down what the organisational pressures, dilemmas and dynamics really are? Might it then be possible to provide new leaders, their bosses and colleagues with meaningful support that could improve their chances of success? So the team began in-depth research work tracking leaders, their bosses and their teams in eight different "case study" organisations for a year. Given the context in which it was taking place, the team decided to use a research methodology known as "collaborative enquiry"; over a one-year period, research team members were "flies on the wall" in team meetings, one-on-one discussions and conversations by the coffee machine.

What really made the difference in transitions?

Analysing and making sense of the data took place in two stages. The expanded team wrote and published a first research report in 2003, which documented the eight case studies and provided some "rough-cut" conclusions (see Binney et al, 2003). In late 2003, Richard Elsner and Gilles Amado decided to return to the material and to extract new insights about the factors which had been decisive in the leaders' transitions. To help them to do this, they conducted lengthy "one year on" interviews with selected case study leaders, and then applied the proverbial "wet towel" treatment to themselves. What really made a difference in these transitions? Was there a set of fixed behaviours, applicable across all contexts, which led to success or failure? Palpably, no. Then what?

To seek to answer this, Richard and Gilles, supported by colleagues in HEC/CPA in Paris, developed the idea that how leaders balanced a number of "polarities" in transition could go some way to explaining what made a difference across a range of different contexts. A "polarity" is basically two complementary dimensions, which are also in tension, which need to be appropriately balanced for the context. A typical "polarity" which all of us at work need to balance is between "work life" and "home life" – the two are interconnected, but also in tension. What happens in one influences the other. Richard and Gilles returned to the case study leaders, and a range of other leaders in the private and governmental sectors, to find out whether these "polarities" were meaningful. Did these help to shed light on what their experience of transition had been? Definitely "yes"! Would knowing about these "polarities" in advance of, and during, a transition be helpful? Possibly! Richard and Gilles's work was published in France in June 2004 (see Bibliography).

The possibility of change: Learning with leaders as they go through transition

In 2004, Bridget and Richard decided to make practical use of their research work of the years before, by creating an organisation which could provide precisely the support they believed that new leaders in post needed, but which was not available anywhere else. So they created The Turning Point with three other colleagues (Jo Howard, Geoff Mead and John Roscoe) to "help leaders to succeed in taking on demanding new roles, inspiring their people and integrating their organisations." The foundations of the practice of The Turning Point are the two research projects mentioned above, to which we are adding ongoing research with transitioning leaders we currently work with.

Since its launch in January 2005, The Turning Point has been supporting new leaders in post to have faster, more successful transitions. How do we do this? We "accompany" leaders through the first six months in their new role – both within their organisations and off line. In these six months, we give them the tools and skills to lead in their new role. Many of these tools have been developed directly from the two research studies mentioned above. Throughout, the leaders are in the company of a peer-group of other leaders from a range of organisations who are in the same boat: they exchange approaches, thinking and practice and broaden their perspective on what it calls for to "take charge" successfully. Our psychologist, Dr John Roscoe, adds fresh insights into the leader's preferred approaches and how these will serve him in the new role.

And the research goes on ... and on ... and on ...

Most importantly, we continue to research leaders in transition. We start our research from the moment a leader joins us, and track his transition with his boss, with colleagues and with him. To conclude, we conduct in-depth interviews with the leader three months after the end of the programme. Three months further on, the leaders of each programme reconvene to review their progress as leaders. Through this research we are also expanding what we know about the role of bosses and other sponsors for transitioning leaders and how teams can enable their new in-post leader to succeed more quickly.

All of the concepts and tools that you will find in this book have been found to work by real-life leaders in transition. Many of these are new and have been developed in the course of The Turning Point's work and have been proven to work in very exacting circumstances. All of the quotes you will find distributed throughout this book come from leaders who have wanted to expand the knowledge available on transitions.

Incidentally, the concept of "polarity" described above has been retained in this book (see section 3), but is described as a "tension" – this term speaks more readily to practising managers. All seven "polarities" from the 2004 book have been retained as "tensions," and an eighth has been added from direct experience with leaders in 2005.

Change and transitions ... go together like a horse and carriage ...

All leaders in our research were being asked to lead significant change: in fact it became clear that leadership today is synonymous with the leadership of change. We couldn't have a conversation with leaders without the topic raising its head. So in addition to finding the themes and core hypotheses about transitions, we also had to look deeply into our research for the assumptions about change that were implicit in the experience of our leaders. These assumptions act like the background of a picture, shaping how we see the figures in the foreground.

They have been distilled not only from our research but also from our working observations of what leaders have to deal with in handling their transition well. The list is probably not exhaustive, but it does describe change as both systemic and strategic – both founding principles of senior leadership roles. Because transitions are both personal *and* systemic, our assumptions reflect the human and the task world that leaders enter into on their first day.

1 **Change is constant, but accelerates and slows down at different times.** Sensitivity to the nature and pace of change in the organisation is part of the important early reading of the context. Remember: few organisations would publicly want it known that their pace of change should be measured and thoughtful: the only game in town is faster than yesterday. Leaders need to know where is the organisational *tolerance* for fast and where might be the organisational *need* for slower. Both are valuable. When leaders are able to successfully read the context of change and be in tune with the organisation's change "melody" – they are better equipped to make the decisions about how and what to change.

2 **To lead organisations through change, leaders need to affirm who they are and be open to changing themselves.** In section 2 on the reality of transition, we describe how winning the mandate to lead and the awareness of the leader's own internal "compass" contributed to personal credibility and the winning of a committed followership. Neither of these elements was available to leaders whose self-knowledge was low and whose readiness to open themselves to others was limited. Taking risks to show who you are, to be vulnerable to being seen as someone who is human rather than superman, were attributes which contributed significantly to the success of the transition because they are so key to contact with others, forging relationships and building trust.

3 **Both the leader and the organisation need to hold the appropriate balance between the need to be who they are and the need to adapt.** Core to our knowledge about how leaders and organisations engage together in a transition, is the belief that both bring proven value and benefit to the other. On the whole leaders are chosen because their experience and who they have demonstrated themselves to be in their career are of direct, tangible value to the hiring organisation. And vice versa: successful leaders choose to join organisations which also hold promise and opportunity – even though sometimes that promise is no more than an echo and the reason for the leader joining is to convert it into a shout. The skill for the leader and the organisation is to know what and where to adapt and what to maintain as it is, so that the best of each is not lost in the tumult of transition.

The new leader enters an organisation that is already "in flow"; initially the leader joins the organisation – not the other way round. Truly appreciating its nature – of adapting, its resistances, its inter-connectedness, how it really functions in practice – is essential knowledge for a successful transition; this is the deep understanding which many new leaders would prefer to quickly skip over and get into changing things so they can demonstrate value and contribution. Balancing appropriately the time it takes to develop understanding with the need to act is one of the most important areas that both the leader's boss and his team can help with.

4 **There are challenges in every transition that are pre-dictable and those that are not – self-awareness supports us to know which is which and respond accordingly.** In this book you will find a roadmap of what you can typically expect in transitioning to a new role. We know this is a likely description (but not necessarily exhaustive) of what some of your experience is likely to be and we also know that some or all of the 8 Tensions are likely to be the core dilemmas you will need to resolve. Whilst predictable, these experiences are not inevitable; the value of a transition roadmap is to alert you to the options for handling these events, to give you some foresight into what might take place and so some advance notice of how you will want to tackle such chal-lenges. But a well-tuned self-awareness, a deep and fearless understanding of who you are is one of the best tools for handling the surprises and turbulence of the new situations, people and events you will be meeting.

5 **Changing jobs is both a life event and a set of practical tasks.** As a **life event** a transition raises questions about the coherence around which the leader has built his image of himself. As a set of **practical tasks** it raises questions about the leader's ability to learn and how he does that consciously. Few of us have ever taken the time to learn about how we learn. We go through whatever education we had and come out the other end variously equipped to get into a life of work. We have seen how a transition is both a challenge to your ability to choose the right things to do, and a time when your confidence about who you are is also under significant threat. Working on both these fronts simultaneously is part of how new leaders manage themselves through transitions well. Doing so involves knowing how you learn about what is going on around you and within you: how curious you are about yourself in this experience of transition and how you convert your curiosity into insights about yourself and your organisation. This is where your readiness to be surprised about what you find in your new organisation and your beliefs about your own need to learn, lend power and credi-bility to you as a transitioning leader.

How to use this book

Don't call us, we'll call you

You may have read this far and be wondering what all the fuss is about. After all, you have changed jobs many times and never had any trouble at all. It's just a case of getting on with it and not making mountains out of molehills. You may firmly believe that leadership today is far too self-indulgent and focused wrongly on who the leader is, rather than solely on what he can achieve and deliver. You may also believe that fundamentally little really changes in organisations: you will always have to handle tricky people issues; the markets will decide whether you sink or swim; involving people more in determining how and what they do at work is one of the reasons everything takes so long; and efficiency and profit are the principal goals to which your efforts should be directed. If this describes your view of the world, thank you for picking up this book and getting this far. But we are not for you.

Skimmers, dippers and flickers

We don't know many people who read books like this from title page to final page. Usually, the world divides into people who like to skim the lot, dip more deeply into what catches their eye or flick over several topics. Whatever your preference, here is what you can expect from the rest of the book.

Section 1: The myths of transition. The common, and frequently accepted, myths and stories surrounding transitions which disable and silence the new leader from dealing more effectively with taking on a new role. Spotting these for yourself is the first step to a more effective arrival in a new post.

Section 2: The reality of transition. We describe the internal and usually silent and secret reality of taking on a new role through the three phases of: Arriving, Surviving and Thriving. Then we identify the 8 Tensions which new leaders are faced with when they join any organisation. We show how these work in practice and how the context determines where the balance for each can be found.

Section 3: The tensions of transition. We will tackle the principal tensions of transition – that is, the more or less visible dynamics which leaders wrestle with in transition and which determine how things work out. In this section, we will describe the dynamic factors which leaders balance in transition and which determine their actions. What leaders do, obviously shapes the success or otherwise of their transition.

Section 4: The inner qualities of leaders. In this section, we explore the inner qualities that leaders can develop to enhance their ability to succeed in transition, and beyond.

Section 5: The tools for transition. Here is a range of tried and tested tools to help navigate your way, boost your skills and expand your thinking through the typical dilemmas and questions of a new role. You will find suggestions on how and when to use the tools.

Conclusion: Leaning into the slope – Thriving on transitions. We finish by drawing out the core capabilities of transition – those things that make a difference if you do them well to how well you succeed in leading through a new role.

And finally ... the roll of honour

This book would not exist without the generous participation of dozens of leaders who have been prepared to let us into their lives, organisations and teams at a particularly vulnerable and delicate time: as they were entering a new role. Their honesty and directness as they reflected on what they were experiencing is captured in the book just as they said it – in their own words. These verbatim extracts bring a vividness to our efforts to describe transitions and bring to life many of the ideas we are putting across. We are enormously grateful for their involvement in our research and for continuing to work with us to develop useful practices for transitioning leaders. In the interests of confidentiality, we have decided not to name the individuals – but you know who you are!

The writing of this book has itself been quite a transition for us through which we have experienced many of the same emotions that new in-post leaders also go through: we have been challenged, stimulated, disheartened, excited, dismayed and refreshed by a host of different people. Closest to us in this enterprise have been our respective partners: Rob Farrands and Mechtild Beucke-Galm who have provided insights, sounding boards and much needed bolstering at those times when our self-belief was flagging.

Surrounding us professionally has been an exceptional group of friends and colleagues. We appreciate Dr Geoff Mead for his wicked sense of humour and stubborn determination that how people learn is a significant differentiator for a satisfying life; Geoff also brought to us a deeper appreciation of how stories and their telling can be used in times of transition and has helped to shape our research strategy. Jo Howard has made sure that we not only pay attention to our work but to ourselves as a group of people needing to model what we espouse for others. Jo's tireless interest in people and what makes them tick has taken her into a frontline position in researching the lived experience of leaders in transition which keeps our research base bang up to date. She has also brought us her considerable experience in the bookselling and publishing industries and acted as our agent for this book; she continues to foster her network in these arenas through regular party-going. Dr John Roscoe has added enormously to our appreciation of what transitions involve personally for leaders. His depth of experience as a psychologist working with leaders in a range of organisations coupled with his talent in designing tools which will get to the heart of the transition experience has been a significant addition to the practical help we can offer leaders. Gordon Sinclair brings years of first-hand experience as a developer of leaders in major organisations, plus a sharp eye for what will work and what will never fly.

We are fortunate to have found a talented group of associates who share our fascination with leaders and their transitions. They have brought their diverse experiences alongside ours and truly made the whole greater than the sum of the parts. They are Marion Gillie, Penny Hamer, Annie Medcalf, Howard Miller, Grahame Pitts and Louise Sibley. Simon Cavicchia has combined his practice of psychotherapy with his experience as an organisation consultant to bring us fresh insights into how leaders handle feedback and continues to work with us on our Master Classes.

Bridget was significantly helped in the early days of her research by the enthusiasm, contacts and practical support of Zoe Morgan whose own life as a very successful senior leader overtook the time she could devote to further work together. Other organisational leaders who have contributed invaluably and in practical ways are: Stephen Battalia, Brodie Clark, Liz Davis, Richard Hatfield, Deborah Loudon, Sir David Omand, Jeremy Oppenheim, Sir David Pepper, Jonathan Potts and Kathryn Wainwright. Rob Morgan has been a challenging questioner in our marketing, managing to find every time the questions we have found too difficult to address and held our feet to the fire whilst we do so.

Gilles Amado has brought us valuable insights into the private, internal world of leaders and was co-author with Richard of a work on transition published in 2004. In that book and in this one, we have continued to use a core idea, which came originally from Barry Johnson, on the management of dilemmas. Barry has worked with us to deepen our understanding of how leaders work through polarities – always with a generosity of spirit and desire to share his enormous accumulated experience. Edwin and Sonia Nevis have both been a continuous source of quiet inspiration.

We would finally like to thank Martin Liu, our publisher at Cyan/Marshall Cavendish, for his grace, encouragement and confidence. Knowing he was there, patiently waiting and encouraging us was a great spur in our darkest and most blocked hours. Thank you.

We want to know whether this book was of interest and use to you, and in which ways. Please send your message to both:

Richard Elsner (richard.elsner@theturningpoint.co.uk) and
Bridget Farrands (bridget.farrands@theturningpoint.co.uk).

1

The myths
of transition

Everyone loves a good story. In fact we tell and listen to stories every-day in some form or other: when we gossip, write a report, pass on a rumour, make an excuse for arriving late, chat around the coffee machine, listen transfixed to the latest on the grapevine, make a presentation, talk about the journey to work. Stories help explain and make sense of daily life, they highlight what is important to us and to others, they surface the heroes, fools and villains in the workplace and they give us a shared "shorthand" for understanding our experiences.

So why does a book about the transition into a new role begin with a section of myths? Myths have been described as:

> *Traditional stories accepted as history which serve to explain events and cultures. They are stories that explain the origins of current phenomena. They may be believed literally or figuratively, or as metaphors about the workings of the world.*

As we will see in the following sections, moving into a new role (and even more so if it is also a new organisation) makes considerable demands on self-confidence, on our ability to live with ambiguity, on our tolerance for complexity and not knowing all we need to immedi-ately, on our courage to ask tough questions and on our need to appear competent at all times. Just one of these can be a tall order to deliver, but if you are expected to fire on all these cylinders, how will you do?

Enter the myths, the stories that help to explain this turbulent time by giving us some simple reference points to steer ourselves through the crazy feelings of disorientation that often come with new jobs. But as you will know from the stories you tell and the ones you listen to, a story doesn't tell the whole truth. You pick out what you want others to know is important to *you* about your experience. The stories and myths that circulate in organisations are no different: they are "short-hand" editions of experience, selectively highlighting certain aspects and ignoring others. But the difference between the personal stories we tell to each other and organisational stories that circulate more generally, is that no single person is choosing what gets included and what gets left out of these.

The stories that circulate about transitioning into a new role are just as prone to this kind of cultural infection. They are selective: nobody chooses consciously what to include and what to leave out, but somehow the stories only seem to carry some of the reality of our experience. Many have caught the bug of "hero leadership" – the leader who apparently takes on the world single-handedly, conquers it despite overwhelming obstacles, brings order where there was chaos and rides off into the sunset, handsomely rewarded by grateful shareholders. Many of these transition myths have become abbreviated to such an extent that they almost parody the reality they are trying to describe. The usefulness of simple messages such as make your mark early on, decide your strategy within the first three months, fire the organisational deadwood in the first month, is very limited when few real experiences of transition into new roles live out these kinds of "truths."

In the following pages, we have taken the commonest myths about transitions and matched them against the lived experience of leaders taking up significant new roles. As you will see, there is usually quite a gap between the prevailing myth and the experience: then we have used leaders' own words to realign the myth so that it more accurately and realistically describes what you can expect from significant issues in transition.

Yes, everyone loves a good story but let's make sure that when you take on something as important as a new role you are using the right stories to guide your experience.

The myth of openness: Leaders can find out whatever they need to know

Few organisations appoint new leaders on a whim: finding and getting in place the right people is an expensive and time-consuming job. So how can this be a myth of transition? Surely the new role comes with a clear mission? And if it doesn't why now wait till it is clear?

To answer these questions we need to look beyond the leader and into the wider organisation. We need to realise that surrounding some roles and some parts of any business are undiscussables: those things that everyone knows but no one dares speak about. A corporate version of the emperor's new clothes. It is often the undiscussables that help the development of myths – people need to find ways to explain what cannot be openly spoken about so myths are a useful shorthand.

Spotting the undiscussable issues

Often the issues that cannot be discussed carry a long history. They stretch way back before any of the current players on the stage were around, but people learn quickly what can be challenged and opened to debate, and what has to be left alone and not discussed. Somehow the history has surrounded the issue with a hushed, untouchable quality that only the extremely brave or the very stupid would dare to broach. And since new leaders are keen to understand and gain acceptance into their organisation they will understandably prefer to conform to the prevailing behaviours and leave the touchy issues well alone. So if everyone behaves as though it's perfectly clear what the leader is there to do, even though he may not be, it's often easier to carry on as though it were clear to him too. Those around the leader collude with the view – usually tacitly because of course it can't be spoken about – and so the potential for challenge is missed again. The ultimate watertight sealing happens when everyone also knows that talking about how this issue can't be spoken about is also forbidden!

Let's look at a few examples:

- A leader who was handed a successful sales operation following the retirement of a long in-post sales director only to find that his first year of leadership saw sales plummet to all-time lows. Nobody would want to talk about how the final year of the last leader was spent frontloading sales contracts so that he could retire in glory, leaving a legacy where the next year could only yield disastrous results.

- Or how about the global manufacturer, market leaders in a certain type of food, who brought in a new leader without letting him know that the market was about to collapse, but continued to insist his job was to perform as though the market were as robust today as it was three years ago?

- Or the new HR leader asked to transform the function across a major UK business, struggled to do so for many months until she realised she was up against an expectation that she would leave out of her plans a significant area of the function? This was led by a long-serving senior manager who had "grown up" with the then CEO who "protected" him from any change.

The myth of knowing and certainty

There is another type of uncertainty that new leaders have to face that is often only discovered after appointment. And this is the realisation that the real role is not the one they were brought in to do. An accident of appointment you might say … easily happens when things are changing fast. But renegotiating the role can be hard when new leaders are already trying to get to grips with multiple other factors and the "what does he really know yet?" is the silent question in the minds of others around him. We do not suggest that organisations appoint people without care and thought: we do know that the complex nature of the context of many senior roles and the difficulty of confronting some of the deeper-seated issues of culture combine to produce less than clear missions for leaders. Then their own reluctance to name their lack of clarity (Is it me? What am I missing here? Just need to do a bit more analysis on the issues ...) compounds the issue and the myth of openness is alive and well all over again.

One leader, Simon, fought hard to get a COO role of another business unit within his organisation, where commercial success depended on working highly collaboratively with two other sister business units. He had watched with dismay and disbelief from his current role at how these businesses had declined and he knew he could make a difference there. He got the job and set to work with energy and conviction. After about three months he began to get frustrated with the pace of change and the lack of visible effort from others so he went to speak to his boss. It was an uncomfortable conversation: Simon couldn't put his finger on what, but he felt something was being withheld. Fast forward – with much further impatience and frustration – another two months and Simon uncovered the reason for the sluggish efforts of his organisation: the two CEOs of the other businesses were at war with each other. Neither agreed with the operating model and each had different alternatives they believed were the right ones. The impasse was stifling all three businesses but nobody dared to name the issue. Instead the blame was put at the door of the culture and the too distant Asian parent of the UK businesses. The real role the COO had been brought in to do was, yes, to build the business but to do that by working around the two disagreeing CEOs. The chances of success about equal to running a marathon wearing Wellington boots.

The reality for newly arriving leaders is to recognise that there are many certainties as they take up their role, but what gets left unsaid is also part of it. Understanding the context, being able to read the subtle signals that all is not as it seems and having the courage to ask awkward questions are ways to explode the myth and check out what *really* are the certainties of the role.

The myth of fast direction: New in-post leaders need to be decisive about setting direction early on

In the myths of knowing and certainty we saw how strong the need is for new leaders to appear to others to be in charge of all they survey: hesitancy, deep enquiry, testing out hypotheses and holding off from too many decisions too early are all seen to be far too tentative and unassertive. Add to that the need the leader himself arrives with: to make his mark and stamp his authority firmly on the new role early on. Already here is a powerful cocktail of ingredients for living out the myth of fast direction.

This myth comes from the assumption that one of the most important jobs any new in-post leader can perform is to provide people with a destination and a direction of travel. We know how important it is to have a direction: 500 or 5,000 people with no alignment of their activities are a recipe for mayhem. But if you have just arrived in the role – and even more critically in the organisation – how will you know whether north is more profitable than the value adding westerly direction? What if south turns out to be the true place of maximum shareholder return? The pressure on new in-post leaders to get on with direction giving is immense. Some new leaders arrive knowing that this aspect of their operation has been put on hold till their appointment, adding further "hurry up" demands to their emotional and mental in tray.

After a few weeks many new leaders describe how far away the *actual* role is they end up doing from the role they were "sold": the reality of the role from the inside is very different from its packaging. This is not from any intention to mislead, but comes from the difficulty of accurately describing the true complexities of leading and managing any operation, especially if the primary job of the leader is to bring about significant change of some kind. And almost all leadership roles today take for granted that they will involve leading change: expansion of markets, shifts in culture, shortening product cycle times, making ways of working more efficient, outsourcing ... the list is endless. Without a deep understanding of how the operation *really* works – which takes time and often different approaches to finding out what that means – how can a new leader provide the right direction for the future and know how change needs to happen?

The alternatives to this myth are not to sit at your desk and wait; nor to arrive with your own convictions of what "this business really needs to do is ..."; nor to unquestioningly believe the analysis given to you by your boss, analysts' reports or industry pundits. We know of a director who arrived in a new role in a sector that was entirely different from the past 20 years of his career. He started a journey around the organisation – literally all over the country – asking just two questions repeatedly for nearly five months:

- If you were in my position, what would you do now?
- If I could say exactly what you would like to hear, what would it be?

And what he learned from these two questions was encyclopaedic: how ready the organisation was for change, how others expected him to lead it, where they thought the business should be going and so what their assumptions were for the future, what they thought of the current strategy, what was really holding the business back and more and more and more ... Here was a leader who had enough confidence and conviction to refuse to be rushed, who knew that providing direction was so crucial it deserved a more profound enquiry than buying into other people's views of the world. He was patient, open, attentive to how things are now, able to hold many and contradictory points of view. In our experience, there are few situations which are so desperate commercially or economically that they need this myth to be lived out.

Here is a different experience of a leader dealing with the crucial question of direction and speaking about it as something that "bubbled up" after nearly six months in a new role:

> [Security is] one of many threads actually. We have around four or five that have emerged and they have only just emerged. I never had an "a-ha" moment ... I wish I had, but they just kind of bubbled up. One of them is the common security issue; the second is we share across the region a common question about how is it that political reform is going to proceed in the Arab world? We share that all together and a common set of issues that are broadly similar in ... most of the countries we deal with ... because ... we do have a remit for covering lots of other countries although we don't have offices there ... So there's the Arab reform, the political reform question; there is the issue of working very closely with other government departments, which we have to do more than most, and in a joined up way.

Both these examples illustrate the way the culture of the operation and the style of the leader intersect, so that direction finding is an activity which emerges from a process of living with the question of "where are we headed?" rather than a task in itself to be ticked off within the first few weeks.

Both these leaders built firm ground to stand on so that the direction they would ask their organisations to head into were solidly rooted in where they *really* needed to go, and one that people understood and felt committed to. This is not to say that organisations in a real crisis need a similar approach: it may be crystal clear in such situations where they need to be headed – to be sold, slimmed down to a core operation, merged with another – and where the speed of doing this is critical to saving the commercial life of the organisation. What the myth upholds though is how unintended results occur when speed and the leader's need to make his mark quickly are the driving considerations for decisions on direction, not the right decision about the right direction.

The Action Man myth: Leaders know what to do when they take up their role

New leaders typically arrive into a new role with business agendas set, budgets decided and often the team they will be leading also in place. They just need to take up their place, grab hold of the reins and keep the show on the road. They may need a bit of time to understand how this particular organisation does things or how this particular role gets done, but on the whole one organisation is much like another, isn't it? And so the myth of leader as Action Man kicks in: whatever you do, be decisive and take action – ideally within the first few weeks – so people will know you are serious about how you like your part of the business to operate. How does this myth work?

The relief of action

We give highest recognition to what we can see happening and changing around us. We value the tangible evidence that demonstrates leaders are making decisions and taking action that will bring about something different. We want outcomes and results; we expect to see action and activity; we feel good when leaders are being busy and purposeful; we prefer to hear them talking competently and knowledgeably; we need to know they are making a difference. And when we see our leaders behaving in this way, we can relax and believe all is well with their world and ours. Someone is in charge – and more importantly someone is making sure things are happening.

This emphasis on "things happening" is a great antidote to having to think, or watch and notice, or find out more about how things really work before deciding what to do. After all, sitting and thinking, reflecting with others, wandering about, asking questions and looking at how things work doesn't look like much is going on. So if leaders are judged by themselves and by others against their ability to get things done, to change the world they lead, then getting on quickly with whatever that means *is* the agenda they must pursue. The surest way to do this is to assume that this new role, the new organisation, department or team is going to be largely like the last one the leader came from, so to treat it in a very similar way: use the well tried methods of analysis, bring out the familiar approaches to working with the team, get to understand the financial ratios, put together a plan and ... off we go! The flaw is to equate speed and action with decisiveness, and decisiveness with leadership; the pressure on a new leader (self-imposed and expected by the organisation) is to want to show what he is made of ... quickly.

The myth is that action and activity in the early days of taking charge will support the leader to feel competent, will enable him to put his stamp of authority and experience on the situation and will reassure those around him that here is someone who knows what he is about.

Stay with what you know – or risk surprise

Here is how a new CEO of a retail organisation described arriving into the role from his previous position as a Finance Director:

> *When I went into the role, what I found myself doing was concentrating on the areas where I had least expertise so I worked on the team, I worked on the large store format, I worked on the development of the catalogue. The area where I had expertise in project management, where I'd put new systems in and managed integration of businesses and disposal of businesses, I applied these processes and frameworks to the new warehouse but I didn't really concentrate on it because I'd swung as a pendulum all the way to looking at the skills that I didn't have. I felt I had to hone those, and in reality that issue of not looking at the warehouse was also the issue that actually undid the company. So it was because I took for granted that I knew what to do, that I concentrated my efforts maybe on the wrong areas.*

Here is a very honest account of how a new leader misread a crucial event (and which later led to his resignation). Clearly this was an issue that urgently needed attention of the CEO, but the assumption was to problem solve it in the same way he had done previously as Finance Director. All the new in-post pressures were present for this new leader: an urgent, costly problem – one he had inherited – that needed rapid resolution; previous senior experience to know some frameworks and processes to bring to bear on the problem; his attention being drawn to new areas of the business where he felt less knowledgeable and believed he should become more competent.

As this CEO got into his role, he realised that the action he really had to take was to move people's ways of thinking – their mindsets – and attitudes to themselves and the business.

And that team, who are still there, took about thirteen months to bring together, then to begin to work in ways that would sustainably address the deeply-seated business problems they were facing:

> *I had to make wholesale change to get to that point. I found the biggest transition was getting people away from the big corporate mindset to a group of people who really understood and were motivated around the fact that they had a business they could believe in and therefore they could work, and they could see it as theirs, and want to turn it around.*

The reality of taking early action in a new role is that it takes unusual forms and needs different start points. Leaders have to be able to challenge personal assumptions about their new context; to be ready to be surprised; to let go of the need to stamp their mark immediately on events; to be very sure that when they do take action it is the right action directed at the right issue; to broaden the definition of what action means so that apparently less active but equally important behaviours of watching, enquiring and wondering can take place. And all this when the silent demand from those around the leader – and from himself – is get in, get started and make your mark.

The myth of independence: Leaders don't need help

In the hero model of leadership, leaders are people who can do it alone. It's not that they consciously think this is how they have to be – it's just what happens, just how things work best. And there seem to be good reasons why being independent of other people is OK. In fact more than that: often there just aren't the right people out there to ask for help. How have we come to value this level of independence so highly? What goes on to make it hard for a leader to shake off the idea that asking others for support is something to be done very carefully and selectively?

Let's be clear what we mean here when we talk about help and support. We are saying that the demands on a person taking up a new role are extensive – both professionally, organisationally and personally – and that these demands are far harder to survive and flourish in without appropriate help. Support means different things for different individuals: it could involve talking through what is happening as a way of making sense of it; checking out intended actions to see if anything is missing; putting words to turbulent feelings; normalising new experiences; taking breaks to get a fresh perspective. Support involves re-energising ourselves when we feel exhausted by the demands of new situations, people and contexts – however we need to do it. So who and where to turn to? Most places seem to have limitations ...

The leader's immediate team report directly to him, so asking them for help won't work because it's not appropriate to get too close to your team – and interestingly asking for help is seen as being vulnerable. The apparent risks for the team are that they see their leader leaning on them, relying on them for knowledge and answers. In hierarchies we expect to look upwards and see only the most able and most strong thriving there. It disturbs our sense of how the organisation is ordered if more senior people are looking to the less senior for guidance and help.

So how about the leader's peer group? This is another group that's difficult to access. Most peer groups contain high levels of implicit competition with each other and the need to sustain, at least, the appearance of independence is strong. This is the group against whom leaders compare themselves; the place where the pyramid of the organisation narrows and future opportunities will become fewer and probably harder fought over. Who can be trusted here – really trusted enough to confide in?

The leader's boss is someone few leaders turn to with requests for help. This is the person who recruited the new leader, the person who was most closely "sold" the benefits of hiring this person (usually by the leader himself) and the person who was responsible for "selling" the job with its many advantages to the leader. It's as though there is a veneer of appearances that mustn't be disturbed and if they are the whole idea of who the leader is will dissolve – he will be found out for who he *really* is. Now if the leader has to ask for help, what will the boss make of him? Not up to the job? Did I make the wrong decision?

Should I have told him more than I did about what he was really coming in to? So the risk of going to the boss – and the risk for both the boss and the leader – is that this might open out a far larger conversation than either wants to have. No, best keep away from the boss.

But there are times when the myth of independence is shattered by the presence of someone who upends all the stereotypes and breaks through the rituals of who can really talk to whom about what. Here is the description of one new leader and the experience of his boss:

> *He's easily the best manager I've ever had in my life by a long way. He's very approachable and we get on well and he's hugely supportive. He's very good with people. One thing I like is his proportionate responses, he's kind of emotionally [intelligent] ... In the past I've often had people who were bullies as bosses or not very good people managers. Some years [ago] I went to a research organisation where I was originally deputy director and then director. When I was deputy director I had a manager, a director who was genuinely a bully. The thing I like about Peter is he is really reliable, he is emotionally proportionate, he has very good emotional antennae for what's going on with other staff and responds to that ...*

Here is a description of what support looks like to one leader. It's clear what he values and the kind of support this boss provides: an emotionally mature and fair response to people, reliability and consistency and someone who doesn't make problems for others. How would you describe your new boss? At this stage, what has been the type of support you have had from him and what would you like that has not yet appeared?

New situations throw up new kinds of risks as leaders work out what to do, how to operate and get to know who they are working with. Dealing with all this means drawing on self-supports such as inner resources of self-belief and self-confidence, stamina and resilience. It also means drawing on outer resources: the areas of support that other people can bring when they are asked for help and when leaders are prepared to balance the myth of their own invulnerability and independence with other characteristics, such as curiosity, challenge to their own mindset and straightforward requests for help.

The "boss's buddy" myth: New leaders and their bosses show up as one

The first day of the new leader arrives, eagerly awaited and slightly dreaded in equal measure by his future colleagues. A short meeting has been arranged at which the executive board member responsible for this area of the business has asked to say a few words. Twenty or so invitees congregate in the meeting room, sharing rather a nervous jocular mood as they await the senior people. The board member walks briskly in, followed by the new leader and the head of HR. After a few minutes of shuffling about between the three to find their rightful places in front of staff, the board member launches forth:

I know how glad you will be to see Jonathan here today. It has been a long wait for all of you since Paula left us, which has meant that a number of you have had to cover off some key areas for me in the meantime, for which I am very grateful. Thank you all for your hard and successful work during these trying times.

One of the reasons why it took so long for today to come around is that we on the board wanted to make absolutely sure that you got the very best man in the field, so we left no stone unturned and our head hunters crawled under quite a number too [laughter] to find him. That very best man is Peter, I can assure you. Because of who Peter is, because of his excellent track record and because of his credibility in the market, I want you to know that he has all of our support. Let me repeat that, in case the message was not clearly received, Peter has all our support and we have very high expectations of him as your new leader. Because I have made this abundantly clear to him, Peter knows that he can come to me at any time of day or night – well, not quite, I am after all the author of the company's new work/life balance policy! [laughter] – for support and back-up if things get tough, as they sometimes do ...

This is a fictional case, but based on several accounts of real-life situations. It speaks to the fact that most employees commonly believe that new leaders have the support of their bosses, and even their loyalty. If not, why would the bosses have appointed them? Surely, the bosses would have absolutely no interest whatsoever in allowing their new leaders to fail! It all makes abundant sense that the bosses appoint people they believe can hack it, and that they will do everything in their power to ensure that these leaders make a success of their new role. The support from on high can only be as hard as granite.

Support comes with conditions

The reality is that many new leaders have to cope with very conditional support from their bosses, and in some cases the withdrawal of it early on. The lack of support from above is one of the main causes for the wavering self-confidence of many leaders, which can put a blight on their experience of leading as well as their capability.

Here is a fairly typical testimony from a leader who has first-hand experience of this:

> *During this time performance was well below target on a key product, and Paul (my boss) was saying "You've got to get credibility." He and I had not been working together for long, and he was not communicating a lot of trust in me. I did not know how to handle that at all. We went in to see George (the Chairman) for the management review and he kind of formally acknowledged that we had been handed a very difficult pack of cards and that's all I needed. So it's really sad all my lows are due to people internally not saying "keep going" enough.*

Of course, not all new leaders in-post suffer from chronic lack of support, but the point is that many do, and that their staff are mainly unaware of it. Managing upwards turns out to be one of the most crucial tasks for the new leader to attend to, because a doubting boss is not a comfortable experience. When a new leader starts to feel that he is in danger of losing the confidence of his boss, this tends to cause him fear and can undermine his confidence. If the leader also feels unsure of his ability to master the complexity of his new role, then an uncomfortable experience can quickly become a very painful one. And this often starts with the leader's boss ...

The "impervious leader" myth: Everything changes but him

This myth is everywhere. It is the myth of the heroic, all-knowing new leader who comes in on a white charger and orders the changes which save an organisation from ruin. It is seductive, and nourished by stories of leaders who have moved mountains and led their corporations to redemption.

This myth is important, because it guides many of the recruitment decisions of new leaders, consciously or unconsciously. The myth follows a largely medical model: an organisation is sick, bereft of solutions and close to death. A new leader is found by a desperate board of shareholders, and he is given extreme powers. He arrives, he meets the people, he quickly sizes up the nature of the illness, and he decides to operate and to remove some diseased body part. He then prescribes some medicine to speed up recovery. The surgery involves factory closures, large-scale redundancies and major financial high jinks. The medicine is of necessity foul-tasting too.

The dispatches from the corporate HQ are at first grim, with evil rumouring of resistance and low morale. Then for what seems an eternity, news of the firm vanishes and little is heard of it. Then, as green sprouts emerge through moss in the spring, the first news of regeneration and successful redirection begin to appear, faintly and without much acclaim. As the months progress, the faint signals become more frequent and louder. Within a further year, solid news of a return to health abounds, and the path to a new life for the corporation is confirmed as being trodden with assurance by a brave, forward-looking workforce.

In this myth, the leader diagnosed the illness correctly, knew what operation to undertake, knew what medicine to prescribe, and he did both in a straightforward, invariant manner. The problem was X. The remedies were known in advance to be Y and Z. Notice what is seen to be static: in the process of administering the medicine, neither the medicine nor the leader is changed. Only the organisation is changed. Once the organisation is healthy again, the leader can leave and seek out other situations where he may apply his knowledge.

This is the myth in a nutshell. Is it prevalent? It seems to be invariably present whenever a leader is appointed to an organisation in crisis, and when time is in short supply. Enormous hopes are placed on the new leader's heroic powers to know the "medicine" and to forcefully apply it, in spite of the pain experienced.

In fact, this myth is one of the most dangerous in our list of myths, because it invites most leaders in the vast majority of cases to drive straight over a cliff. They accept the invitation given to them to be omnipotent. It is very seductive for all parties because we love heroic fantasies of rescues against the odds. We love the "leader as doctor" model, because it is simple and mechanical. The shelves are full of the stories of Jack Welch redeeming GM in the 1990s and will doubtless be so with stories of Carlos Ghosn pulling Nissan out of the doldrums in the early 2000s. The myth conveniently side-steps the fact that for every Jack Welch or Carlos Ghosn, there are hundreds of other cases of leaders who applied the wrong medicine and their enterprises have since disappeared or been taken over.

No medicine works universally

At the simplest level, the problem with the model is that there is no medicine that works universally, irrespective of context. Every situation requires a different medicine, to use that metaphor, and no one leader can in advance know all the medicines. At a more interesting level, the model is dangerous because it presents a simplistic and untrue picture of what effective leaders do. Successful leaders in transition do *not* apply formula – they take the situation they encounter into themselves by enquiry and diagnosis; they are inwardly changed by what they take in, and change *with* the organisation they are leading. They are not "impervious" but permeable and active, at the same time.

Listen to a few experienced leaders talk:

> *I don't think anybody gave me a magic bullet as to how to get through this. I think it was more a question of knowing that I'm not alone and knowing that although this is happening to me personally, actually I'm not the only one in the world that this has ever happened to, and other people have had it happen to them too and they handled it and they came through and have come out of the other side ...*

And another:

> *The leader must avoid becoming a schoolmaster – a giver of lessons. He must not come with the solution. It is much better to get one's staff to express what the nature of the problem is, as they see it, to talk through some options to tackle the problem, to make clear that one does not know what the solution is, and to seek to come to an agreed, shared way forward. Often, I think I know what should be done, and my job though is to hold back from seeking to impose this. My job is to seek to get them to see things my way, and vice versa. As in ... [XYZ pharmaceutical company], I succeeded in my job through influence and proposal-making, rather than through authority, which is more complex. In such roles, one needs to be opportunist and to seek an accommodation between one's vision and what the environment throws up as possibilities.*

The new leader's task in transition is to become a part of the organisation of which he is the leader; to do this, he must balance his need to take others' perspectives on board and to hold his own beliefs of what will be effective in the circumstances. When the leader holds this "in between" position with integrity, his ideas are changed somewhat. He is moving towards the organisation, and being changed by it. Nothing remains unchanged if it is in motion.

The "manly feelings" myth: New leaders in post succeed by being macho

This myth exists largely because so many managers are men. Men tend to see life in organisations as tough, and success in management as requiring toughness. Good leaders are therefore hard and manly people, even if they are women. They are expected to control their emotions tightly, and are not prone to tenderness or vulnerability. New leaders are expected to be decisive in all situations, as men like to be. And if circumstances demand it they can even be brutal. They are allowed to swagger in their role. They distance themselves from others so they are insulated from feeling empathy.

When all around are losing their heads, the leader alone is unflustered and in command of his emotions. We like to think of our leaders in that way because we know how volatile our own emotions can be, and it is comforting that the leader is not prone to them. Because, in our prevalent model of what leaders exist to do, we want them above all else to be able to use their minds to control their emotions, to coolly see how to get us out of a fix or to lead us to success. Leaders are expected to conduct the ultimate victory of brain over emotions, and to use it with calculated precision.

And what do we fear about emotions? We fear that these will divert the organisation from its true unemotional purpose, which is to deliver, come rain, come shine, to its customers or shareholders. We fear emotions, whether fear and anger or joy and love, because these are personal states whereas work is impersonal. Not only do we expect them to control their emotions, we actually expect them *not to feel any*. And leaders appear happy to oblige us in our expectations, by appearing unflappable and poised at all times like a chess player. Leaders don't react emotionally. Full stop. Leaders are not emotional people. Full stop.

Importantly, in this myth, new leaders in-post must not express "female" feelings like tenderness, openness and caring. Those feelings do not belong here. Most male managers fear that expressing emotions, even positive ones, will be perceived as weakness. They fear that, if they reveal themselves to be vulnerable by showing emotion, then others may take advantage while their defences are down.

Emotions are coming in from the cold

Is the reality of today's management like this? In part, yes, but it is changing. Many managers, male and female, are realising that emotions are useful, impossible to suppress and positively contribute to what they bring to the job. In some management teams that we know, the permission to express emotion has transformed how they work. People have become open, listening, understanding and more direct: people become more productive and work happens more successfully.

Here is a testimony from a male leader who has started to abandon the myth, and to develop a new self-perception:

Well actually now you're here you can afford to let go a bit, because people know that you're also caring and sensitive. They know all the other bits about you, they know you're a big tough guy and they know you can do the tough stuff. You've been there and done all that. You're their hero, but now if you can start to show your other side in the context of where you are now, people can see another side to you as a leader. There's real benefit in that, in terms of getting buy-in from the senior team and getting them to do things that maybe they might not have done for you otherwise. Or maybe they'll behave in a slightly different way.

The more new leaders in-post can be themselves, the more likely they are to succeed. To be themselves, they need to make as much of themselves present and accessible to others. That will include feelings as well as thoughts. Some of those feelings will be warm and tender; some of them will be angry and hurt. How much the leader shows of his feelings in any given situation is a judgement call. If forming new relationships is part and parcel of the new in post leader's work, this will be hard to do if he is not prepared to reveal a crucial part of himself – his emotions. People follow leaders they can experience as real people. That means being able to spot in the leader the range of feelings each of us has in our experience of daily lives, ranging from the hardest to the softest. Leaders who appropriately express a wide range of emotions are more accessible and more trusted.

The "100 days" myth: If it's taking you longer, you must be screwing up!

This myth has been gaining ground in the last few years, in line with the increasing pace of professional life, and there is something of a bidding war going on to claim the fastest completion time for transition. Not so long ago, six months seemed to be a pretty fair stab at how long it takes to "get one's feet under the table." Then, the "100 days" fashion took hold again. Some say it started with Napoleon. In 1815, the exiled ruler snuck back into Paris and ruled for 100 days. During the Great Depression, Franklin Delano Roosevelt put thousands of people to work in his first 100 days in office. The first 100 days of John F. Kennedy's presidency included the mettle-testing fiasco of the Bay of Pigs. Now, in his latest and very popular book *The First 90 Days*, Michael Watkins invites new leaders to wrap up their transition, bar a few odds and ends, within 90 days. Where will it end?

The myth holds that if you are aware of what needs to be done during transition and you get to it in an organised fashion, then you can get things completed within three months. The focus is on getting as many things as possible done within as short a space of time as possible. Watkins' and others' works contain exhaustive checklists of "bases to cover" and helpful to-do lists for aspirant leaders. For example, Watkins tells leaders to:

1 Promote yourself
2 Accelerate your learning
3 Match strategy to situation
4 Secure early wins
5 Negotiate success
6 Achieve alignment
7 Build your team
8 Create coalitions
9 Keep your balance
10 Expedite everyone

Given the powerful pressures on time which all organisation workers experience, these recommendations seem to make abundant good sense. The boss, the new colleagues and stakeholders all want the leader to be fully functional as quickly as possible. Who would want to disrupt this bidding war and suggest that three months is just not realistic?

Let's face up to reality

We would. Taking charge of a complex organisation, getting to grips with how the business works, how the organisation functions, what the major strategic options are, what the culture is, how the people think and feel would be a tall order to crack in a matter of months if it were only a matter of *knowing*. But succeeding with transition is a lot more than *knowing* things and people. It is about *arriving* fully in the new context (with all the adaptation and getting-of-bearings required) and then developing the inner stability and sense of direction to *survive*. In section 2, we will describe what we call the "inner experi-ence" of transition where these notions are more fully developed. Beyond the inner experience, completing transition (in our definition) includes having reached full agreement with your boss and your col-leagues on the main planks of your mission and of your approach to it.

While we are reluctant to enter the bidding war in reverse by arguing that it takes *x* or *y* months *more* than 100 days to complete transition, this is our experience: transitions, well completed, rarely take less than a year. Ask the experienced leaders you know, and they will usually tell you that it takes that long before they were really "in charge" and ready to lead.

Here are some quotes from leaders we know:

A lot of this period from the end of last year [when the leader took up the post] until the middle of this year was really getting to understand the business, collecting information, trying to assimilate that information. I'd met a large number of stakeholders, been going outside as well. I talked to private industry so a massive amount of data, and I think probably a feeling that, "So what do I do now with all of this information? Where do we go from here? This isn't right, the structures we've got in place now are nonsense ... What we're doing now in broad terms doesn't feel right. I have all this information which should allow me to decide where we should be going, but I'm so knackered that I can't put the two together." I think that was probably some of the low points in June/July of this last year.

Another leader:

I think probably I finished arriving here, actually, in June, early summer this year, so that's eight months since I began ... It just works very slowly. I think the complexity of the organisation and the degree of change that was needed demand that you take the time required.

We are still in transition, because we could still go in a number of ways in how we deliver the business.

And another:

I look through and I know there's plenty [to do yet] and it's mainly that arriving stage that jinxed it, so I would say I'm between surviving and thriving. [After nine months] I'm well out of arriving; having survived the highs and lows I feel a bit more confident now.

Trying to push the accelerator to the floor with a human process, beyond reasonable haste, leads to failed transitions. A leader and his organisation are through transition when they are equipped, mentally, emotionally and spiritually to climb mountains together. This does not happen in 100 days unless the mountains are very, very small.

2

The reality
of transition

In this section we describe the **internal experience** of transitions: the feelings, silent conversations and dead-of-night musings you have with yourself about what is happening to you as you start and get underway in a new role. We give you the main compass bearings of the first few months so that you can orientate and support yourself in the early weeks of taking charge. This is mostly an invisible world to other people, but a very real one to you. Although few leaders talk about these experiences, they are common to almost everyone starting a new position.

We follow this with a description of the **outer experience** of transitions: what really needs managing and sorting out when you arrive in a new role? Where do you focus first? We discuss the actions that will have an impact on other people and the future of your team, your work and the operation as a whole; we describe the seven areas that leaders have told us are crucial to pay attention to when you take charge.

And in the final part of this section we put together the inner and outer experiences to give you a route map for leading yourself and others through transition.

Taking charge from the inside out

On the first day in your new role, your new organisation (if you have been externally recruited) is likely to have spent close on £50,000 on search consultants to find you and hire you. If you are lucky they will also have equipped you with the tools to do your job – a computer, mobile phone, company car, maybe a personal assistant, desk and office space – adding conservatively another £75,000 to the bill. So here you are, what now? How are you going to make sure the investment in finding you is going to pay off? What can you expect from this important next step in your career – and what can others expect from you? And more importantly, what can you anticipate will be the likely experience of moving into this new role?

Typically, you will have had very little, if any, organised preparation for the role you are moving into. You may have done some preparation off your own bat: visiting stores or branches if the organisation is a retailer or bank; read through recent copies of the company report; checked press cuttings and media reports; accessed publicly available stock market information and share movements, maybe even been to meet some customers. If you are lucky, you will have met the team you are being asked to lead or join, in some rare cases they might even have

Figure 2 Arriving, Surviving, Thriving

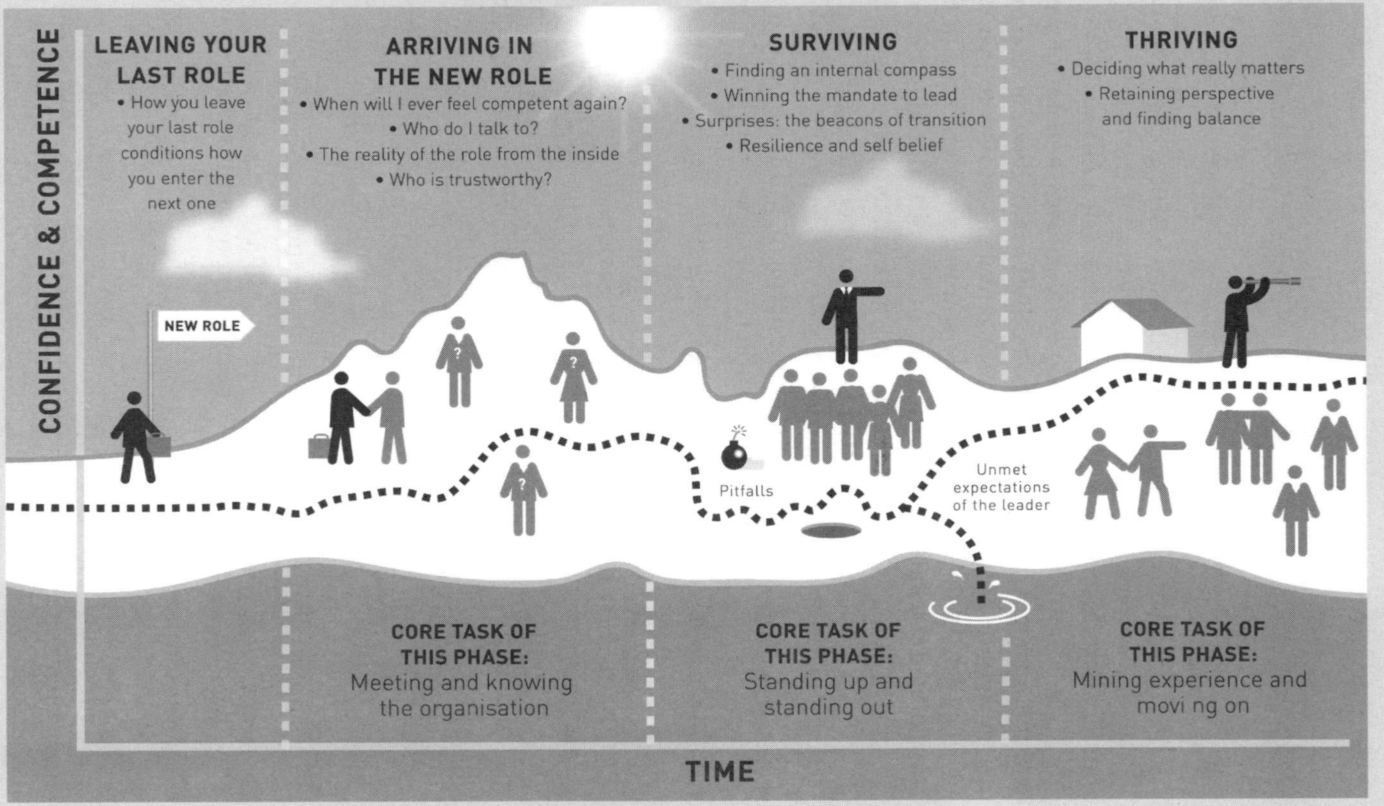

LEAVING YOUR LAST ROLE
- How you leave your last role conditions how you enter the next one

ARRIVING IN THE NEW ROLE
- When will I ever feel competent again?
- Who do I talk to?
- The reality of the role from the inside
- Who is trustworthy?

SURVIVING
- Finding an internal compass
- Winning the mandate to lead
- Surprises: the beacons of transition
- Resilience and self belief

THRIVING
- Deciding what really matters
- Retaining perspective and finding balance

CONFIDENCE & COMPETENCE

NEW ROLE

Pitfalls

Unmet expectations of the leader

CORE TASK OF THIS PHASE: Meeting and knowing the organisation

CORE TASK OF THIS PHASE: Standing up and standing out

CORE TASK OF THIS PHASE: Mining experience and moving on

TIME

been involved in your recruitment. If you are luckier still, you will have visited plants, factories or distribution centres as part of your recruitment. And the most unusual experience of all, your new boss will be there to greet you and host your arrival.

The inside world for you

If this is the picture of the organisation, what will be going on for you? To begin to unpick this experience we have to go to the moment when you decided to accept the job. No doubt you felt a mixture of excitement, anticipation, pride and high self-esteem. Most appointments are competitive so you know you beat off others to win this one: you must have been the best. Maybe you start to think about how to exit your current role well, the farewells, how you will work out your notice, how long the handover will be to your successor. Your thoughts move ahead to the start of the new job and you begin to rehearse what you will do on your first day; who will you want to meet first? What signals will you want your behaviour to send, what messages will other people read into what you do? What announcement will have been made about you – what can you assume others will know about your experience and track record?

Ends condition beginnings

Transitions have different stages and styles of beginning. The transition you experience of starting *into* a new role will have begun by you transitioning *out* of your last role. How you experienced the transition *out* will condition some of how you arrive. If you were made redundant from your last job and it was unasked for and unplanned, then arriving in a new role will be flecked with feelings of relief, gratitude, wariness and caution. You know that if redundancy has happened once it could happen again so don't take anything for granted this time around. If you chose to leave, arriving in a new role will be coloured with high expectations, promises made to you about the scope and content of your new role, opportunities for stimulating, new experiences and plenty of questions. If you have been promoted within your existing company you will probably be making the transition with similar feelings of making a fresh start but mixed with uncertainty about how you will deal with joining as a peer the group who were previously your superiors. And if you are moving into an organisation or role from another country with a very different way of life and even language, you will be facing still more complex feelings as you overlay new cultural experiences with those that come with changing jobs.

The 5 Commandments of Transition

Our research challenges just about all the common practices of taking charge – we call these practices the 5 Commandments of Transition. Here is a recipe that will guarantee you miss out on the surprises and new horizons that job changes can bring for choice and change – both personal and organisational. The 5 Commandments are an invitation to just repeat the last few years of your experience in a new place and with different people: and who is *really* paying you to do that?

1 **More is always better.** Work harder and/or longer – ideally both.
2 **Today and tomorrow are the same as yesterday.** Use your past experience to see you through whatever today throws at you.
3 **Brains rule.** Rely on your intellect to deal with the complexity and newness of what you are facing.
4 **Whatever it needs, change it.** Put your leadership stamp early onto events so you appear "in charge": by redesigning the business strategy, business processes or your own team, for example.
5 **Play the poker hand.** Bluff your way through situations where you feel out of your depth.

We know that whatever is thrown at new in-post leaders is not always something they can handle – at least not immediately – and there lies the opportunity and the excitement. Taking on a new team, new boss, new business, new goals brings many surprises: being open and ready for these surprises and the scope they bring for choice and change is what this book is about.

William Bridges, in his book *Managing Transitions: Making the most of change* gives us this description:

> *Transition is more than simply how we get from* here *to* there, *because it also often presents us with a* there *that we did not expect – a* there *that is shaped by the creative and developmental functions of the transitional journey itself.*
>
> *Actually it is not the fact of being in transition that most people mind, but rather that they cannot place their experience of being in transition within any larger, meaningful context.*

Our research with leaders going through transition has shown that they felt more effective and believed they handled better the situations they found themselves in when they could anticipate some of the inevitable emotional roller coaster they experienced as they began new roles, and when they had what Bridges calls "a larger, meaningful context." It is reassuring to know that what is going on for you is largely predictable, and above all a normal part of a role change. Let's look in more detail at what you can expect from the three phases of transition: Arriving, Surviving and Thriving.

Arriving: Meeting the organisation

What stands out about this phase? Every new in-post leader wants to reinforce the decision to appoint them by appearing confident and competent. Why would you want to be seen in any other way? You will most likely arrive into an already "flowing stream" of business activity which you will be expected to join quickly and effectively. Your orientation or induction is likely to have been short, with an unspoken assumption that "getting stuck in" is the best way to learn the ropes.

After the initial feelings on appointment of excitement and anticipation, other less welcome emotions begin to arrive: low confidence, disorientation, varied success at trying to control overwhelming new complexity, a struggle to get a good read on the business context, self-questioning of your personal capabilities and uncertainty about who are the key players with whom you need to build alliances and relationships.

Key themes in more detail

Personal silence: When will I ever feel competent again?
As a newcomer, people around you will assume that you come with the full armoury of skills, competencies, behaviours and abilities. In fact, everything that could be needed to step in to the job and begin performing. And because you are not likely to want to disappoint people, as well as prove that the decision to appoint you was the right one, you too will probably behave as though you have all you need to perform.

Leaders Speak ...

One day he [the previous leader] went and the next day I moved in here and took over the reins. And it was just a massive, massive change, beyond anything I would have dreamt. For the first quarter of last year, the business was in a dreadful state as well – I had inherited a real can of worms. I would say, probably truthfully, for the first six months, my competence was absolutely smashed because of what I had to deal with and the massive sort of pressure that came with it. And, you start to really question yourself as to whether you are even capable of doing this job.

MD of business unit, global food manufacturer

The tiny prickles of concern that most new hires experience about some aspects of the role they are entering are typically squashed down or get washed over in the tide of excitement and pride of arriving. These often prove to be the very areas where they will need good measures of personal courage in coming weeks: the courage to challenge complacent practices and the inevitable history of avoidance of difficult decisions. But all that has yet to surface as you arrive.

There is a kind of "ecology" that surrounds new leaders, a mini climate zone that is full of optimism and hope. Leaders are invested with expectations and aspirations that are sometimes beyond the ones that even they want to achieve! They embody all that is contained in a fresh start, the power of the new broom to sweep away what has not gone right in the past and to begin to create a new and better future. At least those are the hopes of people around the leader. And depending on the performance of the operation you are taking on, the pressure of these expectations will be greater or lesser.

In the Leaders Speak box you will see how one leader described arriving in the new role. She was under significant pressure to turn around the business she had just taken on in her new role as MD. She is an energetic, confident, highly capable woman with considerable previous experience which would equip her well for the promotion to MD. She knew the business, having come from another part of it, and still the demands of the first six months of the role took a toll on her. The struggle for competence comes about because there is obvious external pressure on leaders to appear and act with competence; it is implicit in the decision to hire you. There is equally strong pressure the leader puts on herself to prove her competence. What gets sandwiched in between both these demands are the confusing and completely unexpected experiences of low confidence, reduced competence and self-doubt. These experiences act like leaking acid out of a battery, corroding the context they come in contact with and sapping the available energy.

Sheltering the truth

So what is the typical response of leaders who go through this common experience? Say nothing. Keep mum. Don't talk to anyone. Don't admit to feeling like this. Nobody acknowledges that feeling your competence is "absolutely smashed" is something that can be discussed. It must remain a secret. Nobody must know that the leader, in whom is invested so much, is struggling. And the struggle is as much with the inner demons of self-doubt as it is with the outside world of turning around a business.

When the MD above was asked why she had not said anything to anyone she said:

> *Nobody wants to let down the person who appointed you; how could I say to [her boss] what I was going through? I needed him to go on believing in me and trusting that I knew what I was doing. And anyway he's someone who believes it's sink or swim so I wouldn't have got a lot from him.*

What do leaders do that works?

✓ Acknowledge appropriately and selectively the parts of the new role that you are finding especially tough. Describe your experience to others as normal and expected.

✓ Don't overplay your optimism or show confidence you don't genuinely feel – people know when leaders put on an act.

✓ Trade on the fact that being new buys you some licence to sound and feel confused.

Crowded isolation: Who do I talk to?

Many of the leaders who took part in our research spoke about how tiring it was to be continuously surrounded by people, how hard it was to find time to sit alone and think and plan. In the early stages of entering a role, choosing who to respond to and who could wait was a judgement call that could be hard to make. The tumult of meetings, new faces, new content, issues to quickly understand and have a view about were part of the enjoyable stimulation they looked forward to, but the constant need to absorb and process new data all day was also exhausting.

And at the same time as they spoke about how crowded was their working day, they also described how lonely and isolated they felt. One leader described it as, "I'm completely alone in an endless crowd." How do we explain the contradiction of crowded isolation? And what makes it worth understanding in the context of taking up a new role? We go first to the leader's inner experience to see what is happening there and then go outside to see what is going on around her.

Who shall I be here?
We have to go back to the need, when arriving in a new role, to control and make choices about how others will see us, what we will choose to show them of who we really are. It's the difference between being on your "best behaviour," when you act deliberately and knowingly to create a particular impression, compared with acting more relaxed, laid back and being who you feel like being at any moment. We know, too, that in situations of uncertainty, many people increase their feelings of "safety" by acting in more constrained and formal ways which increase the emotional and psychological distance between them and others. Whilst distance may help us to feel safer, maybe even more confident, holding other people at arm's length also makes them more remote and increases our own sense of isolation and loneliness. The questions new leaders are silently asking themselves are:

- How acceptable will it be for me to show people here what I'm really like? What might happen if I tried it?
- Who could I trust enough to let my guard down?
- How will I decide?

The question "who shall I be here?" is a fundamental one in transitions. It goes to the heart of choices about identity and who to show up as in this situation. We have an ideal picture – sometimes called a self-image – about the person that we are, one that may not always be fully clear to us but usually one that we can describe well enough when asked. Often this ideal self-picture lurks at the edges of our awareness and we only become fully aware of it when we act "out of character," when we surprise ourself with our actions or choices. New situations are the most likely times when our ideal self-image is questioned. How come the great way I make decisions doesn't seem to go down too well here? I've always been good at making decisions. What is it about the way I like to talk to people that gets an odd reaction? I'm informal and approachable and people usually like that. What's going on here? Probably a clash of context or culture with the person you know yourself to be which needs some kind of adjustment. Clearly a new role doesn't call for you to stop making decisions or not to be approachable. More likely it is calling for you to watch and learn better how this context needs decisions to be made, or what being approachable means here. For you, it will ask that you re-consider who you might be now and how you might need to flex your self-image. New roles ask us to bring ourselves up to date with who we might need to be here and leave behind some of who we were.

Hierarchy, power and distance

If this is what's going on within the leader, what is happening in the environment around the leader that impacts his experience of crowded isolation?

Senior roles carry special power and significance for others. Like it or not, senior people are treated differently from the less senior. We tend to be more careful, more watchful, more cautious in how we behave in the presence of seniority. Hierarchy has a distancing effect. So however accessible you as a new leader decide you are going to be, there is only so far that others will be prepared to come towards you if you are more senior than them. In our research, when we asked leaders how they wielded power and what made them feel powerful, they denied they had any. They felt uncomfortable with any idea that they exercised power. It was as though power was a dirty word that they didn't want to be associated with.

Check out this response of the CEO of a national brewery company when asked: how powerful would you say you are in your company? Notice where he ends up – power for him is simply about intellect, not about position. It may be that for the most senior leader, but for others it will also be position that matters:

> Well, if I'm not powerful what am I? I mean I've got the potential to have power, it depends on how you want to use it. You take a decision and you can get it implemented if that's the way you want to go about things. But it's not my style and it does depend on the individual, though my predecessor had a certain style which would have been described as autocratic and he very much felt that the

decision making would have rested with him and, everything else would have followed from that. In our own structure now, I see my job is to get the team of people to reach the right decisions and it's not about power it's about ... you know, you're there to run a business and a business is all sorts of things, it's the customers, it's the people in the administration, it's the whole caboodle. And you're there in part to make sure that business structure operates at its most efficient and it's aware of what's going on where it touches the customer and so on. And that's not about power, that's about using your brain and information.

So working out how much to reveal of yourself, who to reveal that to and encouraging others to take the risk of being open with you is bumpy territory to begin with, which needs care and sensitivity to navigate well. It repays careful observation of the context you are operating in and a good understanding of what your own values are on self-disclosure and openness. You might have found yourself in an organisation which says openness is important, but struggles to practise this. What do your own values tell you matter to *you* on this question? In the context of your role, how could you behave in a way that is consistent with those values, whilst respecting the (possibly different) behaviour of others?

In the next section on Surviving, we will discuss the importance of leaders showing clearly what they stand for as one of the conditions of followership, and how this works alongside crowded isolation.

Leaders Speak ...
There's nowhere to go, you can't go to your boss with this [transition]. You can't go to your peer group, you can't go to your team — you need an outlet. You need to find a group of people who aren't going to counsel you, but at least could empathise with you and help you cope through the bad times. I don't think anybody gave me a magic bullet as to how to get through this. I think it was more a question of knowing that I'm not alone and knowing that although this was happening to me personally, actually I'm not the only one in the world that this has ever happened to, and other people have had it happen to them too and they handled it. They came through and have come out of the other side.

Senior government operations director

What do leaders do that works?

✓ Find a trustworthy individual away from the operation you can speak openly with about your experience and what you are doing.

✓ Be firm with your diary and what goes in it. Give yourself some thinking time.

✓ Be real about what happens when you become more senior. You feel the same but others see you differently. Work out how you want to exercise your own authority.

Not in the job description: The reality of the role from the inside

When does the newness of changing roles move from excitement to stress? What is the tipping point between *enough* variety to be stimulating and too much that you get exhausted? How do you find that mix of experiences which will be just rich enough to satisfy you, without indulging in such an excess that "experience hangover" is the result? These questions go to the heart of managing this early phase of transition, but are especially relevant to the experience of "role shock": how the role you take on turns out to be from the inside, doing it, compared with the role you were "sold." Rarely is a job offered with the intention to mislead: simply that how the reality of a job is described and sold and how it is brought to life in the doing of it are very different. And here lies role shock.

Organisations can scrub up well

Not surprisingly, trying to find the person with the right mix of expertise, experience and potential is much like the hunt for the Holy Grail. So jobs have to be marketed like any other commodity – the most attractive features highlighted, the status enhanced, the scope just a bit larger than life. Hiring managers also have to put their best self forward: push into the background their tendency to be demanding, impatient and action focussed; bring forward their approachability, tolerance and understanding. The presentation of the organisation you are joining will also be to scrub it up well and dress it in its best suit. Not surprisingly, the process of hiring into leadership roles tries to leave nothing to chance.

You too are marketing: but you are marketing Brand You. Just like the hiring manager you are putting forward the best version of you and your experience. Finding a new leader is like a slow motion version of speed dating: both parties want to show off their best sides, they want to ask the most insightful questions, to probe and challenge the issues which will highlight the best and the worst of what they are going in to. And like speed dating, even the best questions and most rigorous search process can't guarantee that you will find out all you need to know about whether this is the right relationship (job/company) for you. You have to take a calculated decision and then trust that you will be able to make a go of the role. Finding a mismatch between these two dimensions doesn't necessarily mean that you or they have made the wrong decision to hire you. Of course sometimes that happens. The more likely explanation is that this experience is showing you a gap – what William Bridges describes as "a *there* we did not expect" – and it is this gap that invites you into the personal and organisational work of transitions.

What you see is *not* always what you get
What stands out of our research is the shock that many leaders felt at how the "sold" role and the actual role differed. It's a surprise they were surprised, but more useful is to know how this happens. Well, marketing is one explanation – see above. Another is the trap that only revealing our best self gets us into. And the trap is to close off the chance for any real conversation about the less than best parts of who we are, who the others are and what the work is really, really like. "Best" is too shiny, too neat, too limited – it sets up an aspiration that can't be reached. So the result for a new in-post leader is to have to bridge the gap between the sold ideal of the role, herself and her boss and the reality of all those rubbing along together every day. And role shock is the result.

Role shock is not a predictable template you can lay over any new role and anticipate beforehand how it will look. Rather it is the experience of transition where the gap between what you thought you were coming into and what it turns out to be is so wide that you find the differences hard to bridge. These differences take you by surprise because they threaten your self-confidence, competence or self-control and self-image.

Leaders described time demands and time intrusions that they had not been warned about: expectations that they would take business calls late into the evening and Sundays becoming just another working day. Whether right or wrong, this is an increasingly common way of working: why it was a symptom of role shock was because it was not expected or negotiated *and* challenged personal beliefs about where the boundaries of work and personal time should be drawn.

> **Leaders Speak ...**
> Once I got over the shock of how my time no longer seemed to be my own, I made some big changes – as much as anything just to survive. I made some decisions about things I wouldn't do any more. Basically I've cut out everything that is for me. My time is either work time or children time; the starting point is that I put all their school events in red and if they have exams, time to revise with them. I try to have breakfast with the children three times a week and try to put them to bed two out of five nights and I try not to work weekends other than Sunday nights. That all means I often work to 2.00am, but I very seldom work Friday night or Saturday evenings.
>
> *Senior manager, advertising agency*

Another realisation for one leader was finding that her skills of consensus building needed sharpening:

The thing that surprises me most is how hard it is to get things done that you want to get done and also – this shouldn't have surprised me – how much of a matrix world we live in, how little you are actually responsible for or how much you have to influence to get people onside. Everyone says "just do it" but if you do just do it then six people tell you why you can't or shouldn't. So despite the theoretical "just do it," the reality is it doesn't work like that: consensus is necessary.

Other leaders spoke about the gap in their skill set as the role unfolded: they were needing to become adept very fast at managing the politics of influencing. Some described needing to find reserves of patience at the slowness with which decisions were implemented. For others stepping out of the detail and taking on larger and wider perspectives externally were the unexpected areas of their skill gap. Role shock is compounded because new in-post leaders fail to also negotiate what they will need to learn through the new role. The focus is on past achievements and the fit and relevance of history for the current role. Anticipating the future and where the individual's role gaps might be would take hiring conversations into territory that could potentially show off less than the best – of the individual, the hiring manager, the organisation and the role itself – but which would generate a more productive tension between current talent and future potential.

Imagine how different the hiring conversation would be if it had anticipated this experience from a senior leader:

I had to completely set my own agenda. In other jobs there had been people telling me what to do. Here it was up to me – and I had to decide how I would make a difference. That was quite a question for me to be faced with at a time when there were so many other areas that needed my attention. When I think about it now that kind of freedom is what I had always wanted. It was just such a surprise to finally get it.

What do leaders do that works?

✓ After a few weeks in the job, take a long hard look at your capabilities and ruthlessly compare these with the demands of the role. Where you are falling short, put in place immediate development for yourself.

✓ Insist on a progress review with your boss after four, eight and twelve weeks to check on success in arriving, emerging shortcomings and negotiate ways to address them.

✓ Recognise the differences between the "sold" role and the real role and get on with working the real role, without losing too much sleep about what it was not turning out to be.

Who brings the important news? Finding out who is trustworthy

We saw in the Crowded Isolation theme how seniority and power are distancing attributes for leaders. Yet one of the most important ingredients in leading is to have a finger on the pulse of the organisation. For new arrivals, getting to understand how the organisation really ticks is crucial to knowing where support or resistance for change plans is likely to come from. Getting regular temperature checks on morale as well as the significant "stories on the street" all enable leaders to read more accurately the real heartbeat of the operation. Leaders, in part, need others to provide them with this information so finding the trustworthy and reliable sources of information was crucial to their getting a fast and effective understanding of what they were leading.

The expectation that people – especially his own team – would be trustworthy was the start point for this CEO who took over a retail business with significant distribution and supply chain problems. He knew the importance of being in touch with as wide a number of people as possible. He knew he personally had to work at how he did that and the shock for him that, on his doorstep, was a team he could not trust:

> *The one thing that let me down was I wasn't getting proper communi-*
> *cation. I had put a lot of effort into communication. I was very*
> *conscious of not being a flamboyant or natural communicator, so I*
> *had to do a lot of work to hone my skills there. But the thing you rely*
> *on as Chief Exec. is that people will talk to you. Or you hope they will.*
> *So you quickly learn that you have to be in touch with all parts of the*
> *business because the business model was changing as we worked it*
> *through. But the thing that I found from the directors I had on my*
> *board was lip service. A lot of lip service, in terms of "yes we agree."*
> *But actually when tested, they didn't. I had to ask some tough ques-*
> *tions about who was with me and who wasn't.*

Finding the pulse

The key activity for any new leader in the Arriving phase is to under-stand, in the widest sense, the context of her operation. This is more than knowing the business strategy, more than working with her immediate team, more than meeting the bankers and analysts. It is to connect as closely as possible with the heartbeat of the operation. Acupuncturists believe we all have three pulses: one connected to the physical body, one to our emotions and the third connected to our spirit. Organisations also have several pulses – probably many more than three – which new leaders must make it their job to find and feel. There are no shortcuts to doing this. Walking about, talking with diverse groups, checking out hunches and asking awkward questions are the bases of building trust and finding out where the pockets of honesty about the heartbeat of the organisation really lie.

Data like this also enables the leader to know where and how she might also need to change. One of the myths we busted in the previous section was that new in-post leaders are impervious to being impacted by the organisations they join. In reality, both leader *and* organisation are going to be changed by their mutual interaction. This tension is one that different leaders discovered with varying degrees of satisfac-tion and skill and is the crux of this theme in Arriving. How much does the new leader impose her own values, ideas and views and how much does she adapt and flow with what she inherits? How is trust built in the early weeks of entering a role and why does it matter? Let's look at

Leaders Speak ...

I think a mixture of listening to them [the team], taking on board the expertise and experience that they had, but at the end of the day making up my own mind ... I think most of them respect that, even if I disagreed with them, I was prepared to change my mind as well, not on big things but prepared to be flexible. I think the other thing was not coming in from day one saying, "Okay every boss changes things. We're going to change things and this is what we're going to do: a, b, and c." I don't think that would have worked. The fact that I was prepared to come in, talk to them and listen to them about their concerns, about what they thought about things, helped enormously, and that helped to bring them along. I think if I had tried to change things without really understanding the business, or them knowing that I didn't understand the business, I think I would have lost them.

Departmental head, Government ministry

the different experiences of two leaders who entered their organisation with very different approaches and the impact they each had on trust building as a basis for finding out the important news about how the business really operates.

The first example is the new CEO of an international pharmaceutical company – we'll call him Tim Mason – who arrived from the United States to take up a new role in the United Kingdom. The company he was joining had enjoyed several years of sustained growth under its previous CEO. The brief was a simple one: to continue the trajectory of growth by opening up new markets and developing new brands. Clear vision? Sure. Know what we are here for? Certainly. OK – let's go.

Winning people round

But what became clear as the new CEO got his feet under the table – and had not been made clear to him through the recruiting courtship – was that his senior team had a variety of views as to how continued growth would happen. The marketing director thought it would be primarily through driving greater market penetration in existing markets by brand extensions. The manufacturing director thought it would be by outsourcing manufacturing, ideally to the Far East. The R&D director thought they needed more distinctive formulations so they could make better claims of treatment efficacy. The CEO himself was arriving with a track record of success in a competitor company and keen to prove that his experience could be put to good (and fast) use in his new role. In other words, he also believed he knew what was needed to deliver the vision of growth.

Despite visits all around the organisation to talk about how the future could look, he met stalling and resistance. He found it hard to put his finger on exactly what the resistance was about and who it came from; but he knew plans were not happening as they should. His early mistake was to believe that his considerable energy, determination and conviction were enough to generate the will in others to deliver what he wanted. The need for speed and the hungry demands of business growth had overtaken the quieter, less visible processes of listening, watching and allowing others to engage with him. In practice, it took nearly a year for this leader to align his senior team behind a strategic plan which they believed in. He and they took part in some fierce conversations, spoke tough home truths to each other, disclosed personal fears and hopes and finally built up enough trust to know what was important to understand about each other and the business they were running.

Compare this approach with the arrival of a very different leader and how he went about finding out who was trustworthy. Stuart Locke was appointed to revitalise an ailing public corporation. When he arrived he immediately went on a countrywide tour. In this act alone he busted the myths of independence and action man. But he did more to signal that his arrival would bring other changes too. He made internal broadcasts to the whole organisation and was known for personal emails to individual employees. To restore organisational confidence he had to begin with how he acted and show, through his actions, what he also expected of those around him. Senior managers had to unlearn remote leadership and become an active set of collaborators. Before they could ask this of others, they had to ask it of themselves.

Both Stuart Locke and Tim Mason imposed their own approaches on their organisations – with very different results. Locke deliberately set out to reverse some of the existing cultural traits of his new organisation through actions which made him accessible and open to many. He knew, because of the state of the organisation when he took it over, that senior leaders had to set a different example of leadership if they wanted a different kind of followership. Locke learned huge amounts about how his new organisation really did its work and got things done. He was able to sort through what was important to know and what he could ignore.

Tim Mason went straight into delivering what he had been appointed to do with little regard or understanding for the cultural history of his new organisation. His own ambition and need to take a central role in showing that he could do what he said, overrode other more subtle considerations about the value of trust as a conduit and early warning of organisational readiness or resistance. The important news about the organisation – who were the early adopters of new ideas?, what were the sources of pride and shame?, which parts of the organisation were sworn enemies of each other and where did easy collaboration take place etc? – took far longer for Tim Mason to unearth than Stuart Locke. The balance between Tim's internal, personal drive to show what he was made of, overrode the value of sensing out the operation.

Leaders arriving in a new role face good news and bad news. The bad news is not knowing very much about who to trust and the good news is not knowing very much who to trust. Not knowing creates the best conditions for finding out and getting to know who is on the patch. It's the best opportunity to go out and ask questions about *everything* – however naïve and stupid they sound. Not knowing is only bad news when you assume you *already do* know.

What do leaders do that works?

✓ Hold off from making early judgements about people and keep your own opinions about others to yourself.

✓ Recognise that trustworthiness and liking are not the same. Separate the actions that demonstrate trust from personality and style.

✓ Match your approach to the needs of the situation – and use it to shape decisions.

Chaos, clarity and courage: Finding the way and finding yourself

How do we manage what we cannot discuss? We saw earlier in the section on Personal Silence, that few leaders spoke about their experiences of transition to others, and if they did it was usually to do so in the language of coping, enjoying and getting to grips with what needs to be done. Despite the blur of information overload and the temporary fog of confusion, all was apparently well.

What opportunities are missed when the coping strategy is so far from the experienced reality? Do leaders take longer to become effective when they live a dual existence – where the inner experience and outer lived-in world are so at odds? Every leader we have been involved with through their transition has had to decide at some point what they will personally change in themselves. It is never enough to only concentrate their attention on their organisation, although this is the first port of call for most. At some point, sooner or later, they will turn their focus on themselves and, sometimes painfully to start with, begin to question the transformation they want to make of themselves as leaders. What will be the defining shift in who you are that this job allows you to make? If you are to fulfil more than the description that David Whyte uses in *The Heart Aroused* of "employees as highly paid extras there to serve the ambitions of others"– then what opportunities does the chaos of the transition experience offer you?

Crossing the threshold

Leaders make effective transitions when they can find some meaning for what is going on that enables them to cross personal thresholds which enlarge who they know themselves to be. The opportunity to discover qualities and capabilities that their work up to this point has exiled or not given them the chance to know, is part of the satisfaction and deeper reward that many describe. The process of rebalancing the out-of-kilter aspects of themselves, with new insights into their own leadership practice was a way in which many leaders found a new confidence to act differently. Getting to that point needed some pre-conditions:

- Enough curiosity and interest in themselves to explore the questions that the transition was raising about their way of operating.

- Support and "safe places" where they could be open and vulnerable – ideally with other people going through similar experiences.

- A readiness to flex how they knew themselves to be – to allow the past "self" to adapt into a more up to date version shaped by current circumstances.

Julia started her new role in didactic and prescriptive mode, asking for and getting little support from her own team. She believed she knew

> **Leaders Speak ...**
>
> *I was in this job with people to manage – not aware that [managing people] is a whole new thing to have to face. It came to a dénouement about a year after I was in, when just before I was about to go on holiday, one of my team came up and said, "I'm resigning because I am completely confused. I don't know what you want me to do. You're always changing your mind. You're very difficult to work for." I was horrified because I was completely unconscious – a very low level of empathy, I would say. I had no idea I was causing these stresses in this guy's life. So I said to him, "Look, I don't want you to go. I'm away for two weeks, just hold on and when I come back we'll work through it." I then went into a conscious way of learning to manage people, which is a journey that I've probably been on ever since.*
>
> **Head of business unit, food manufacturer**

what had to happen to downsize the function she was leading and merge it with another. She treated the work as a large project of which she was the project manager. Achieving the right result was about getting a good plan in place, putting in stretching milestones and launching people into an organised set of tasks. What she learnt was that she needed to trust her people to know as much or more than she did, to be open with them and to show more of herself as a person, not just as a manager:

> *I'd never really thought of taking over a job as a* process, *especially not as a two-way thing – me taking over a team and them getting a new leader. Before I'd been quite egocentric – just been concerned about myself taking on a new role. The most valuable thing I've learned was the understanding that this is a process – you can do it in a planned way, and make choices about how to do things.*

After some false starts and changes of plan, Julia also came to realise that creating bonds with others does not have to be to the exclusion of other work:

> *If you don't let yourself get passionate, how can you expect others to become passionate? You can't do that through a ten-point plan. You do need the ten-point plan, but to sell it to people you need the vision of where the ten-point plan will get you.*

Another leader, Terry, realised the value of adopting a true position of learning from his people. He became clear that *his* way was not the only way and allowed others to really contribute whilst he listened. He learnt that this approach took longer at the outset, but he believes now this is the only way to lead people to change their organisation. The impact of changing his leadership has meant neither he nor his team is bypassed and they are all seen as having high credibility in the wider organisation.

Our point is not that these are exceptional changes in their own right; more how they illustrate the dramatic shifts experienced leaders have made as they use the chaos of early transitions to transcend the limitations of their current approach and self-knowledge. These are people who have been ready to be rattled by what they saw of themselves and then been wise enough to take such disturbance as a signal for change.

In the Surviving phase of transition, we will explore in more depth how these questions of identity and personal change which begin to bubble up in Arriving, become more insistent and demanding of attention.

What do leaders do that works?

✓ Take deliberate steps to increase your self-awareness of how you prefer to operate.

✓ Recognise that you could be both the problem and the solution to issues. Replace certainty with curiosity.

✓ Find the meaning of the transition for yourself.

Surviving: Standing up and standing out

In this second phase of transition leaders experience a growing confidence in the content of the work and far more familiarity in how to deal with the day-to-day demands of the role. But as one leader said, "Just when think you are out of the woods, they are about to get thicker!" Several features of senior roles seem to emerge at this stage and make subtle but stretching demands of leaders. This is the phase of transition where *who* you are, *what* you decide to show of yourself and *how* you reveal more of yourself are significant in a number of ways in:

- Winning support for change.
- Enrolling followers in work they feel committed to.
- Establishing a style and approach that is believable and beneficial to you and others.
- Enlarging what you know of yourself as a leader.

If Arriving is primarily about immersing yourself in the new role and business context and getting a realistic enough understanding of what that is so that you can begin to act with confidence, then Surviving is about how you allow that context to influence your identity and practice as a leader. We saw in the first phase of Arriving how tenacious the new leader can be in holding on to who he is, what he already knows and how important it is for him to reassure others by demonstrating competence and self-assurance. Because it takes time to immerse yourself in a new context, to put away your preconceived ideas and be receptive enough to absorb what that context might offer you, these questions of identity – who am I in this role? – begin to arise once leaders have enough "head space" to focus on them.

Often the questions were brought to the surface by organisational events (a "state of the nation" address, a request to describe their own leadership) or by a personal recognition that how they had led previously was not going to be enough this time around. Leaders who were prepared to adapt their identity and increase their self-awareness reported significant insights and shifts in their practice of leadership, to the benefit of their organisations and themselves. These were the leaders who refuted J. K. Galbraith's famous assertion:

Faced with the choice between changing one's mind and proving that there is no need to do so, almost everybody gets busy on the proof.

Demands of senior roles in the Surviving phase centred on the clarity of the leader's "internal compass" as a reliable means to steer and guide himself through the new territory of the role and the leader's ability to handle with grace and understanding the extent of his power – both positional and personal. There was also surprise at the constant struggle to make things happen, new understanding of the need for personal consistency and congruence in behaviour and approach – the place of resilience and stamina as qualities which seem essential to achieving almost anything. For some leaders there was surprise and disillusion at the extent of the politics they had to engage with to make things happen, the frustration of juggling all the balls that multiple stakeholders asked of them but also the delight when attempts to work in new or different ways paid off.

Time and turmoil: Throw out the plan

We tend to think of experience as linear in time, following a sequence of events through a year. Although this is a useful way to describe, measure and locate what is happening to us, to put some order onto experience, the reality of felt experiences is far less neat. So the themes you can expect to meet in this next phase of Surviving *may* occur in time after the ones you met in Arriving, or they may happen simultaneously and even prior to some of those in Arriving. Your situation and what you experience is dependent on you, the role, the context and the mission you are given.

The value of an internal compass: Describing a personal "true north"

Transitions always involve jolts and challenges to our perception. One of the reasons they can be disorienting and destabilising is because they ask us to question and confront:

- How we see the world around us.
- How we see ourselves in that world.
- How others react to us.

Whenever we fully engage with those questions, we are faced with decisions about:

- What to hold on to (where to keep me as I am)?
- What to let go of (where do I need to be different)?
- What might be possible for myself that I know nothing about yet?

These questions, about what to change in personal practice, how far to "go out" and take on the behavioural traits of the organisation and what personal attributes should remain constant, are some of the personal decisions that leaders tried to address in this theme of Surviving.

Projection

In the early weeks of transition, it is usual that people around the leader project their own needs and expectations onto him. This process of projecting operates in both positive and enabling ways as well as ways which disempower and disable leaders. It is useful to know how it works because it allows you to resist the negative impacts and to harness the enabling possibilities. First of all, what is it and how do you spot it?

Projection is more than just the *voicing* of expectations. It also involves the unaware transfer of others' own desires and emotions onto the leader, with the expectation that the leader will behave in ways that deliver those desires. In organisations that are struggling to survive or which have ambitions of dramatic change, new leaders are often given almost Messiah status that single-handedly they will turn the situation around. In these cases, the projections of hope, optimism, ability, vision, creativity, influence and energy loaded onto the new leader are huge. No wonder the role can feel like carrying the weight of the world. Implicitly what others are saying to the leader in such situations is, "We want *you* to be visionary, optimistic, hopeful etc because it is not possible for us. Come here, be our saviour and deliver the business." Self-aware leaders resist this call to heroism. In other words, they refuse to accept these projections because they recognise the seduction and trap of such silent requests. They know that the only healthy way to bring about sustainable change is to enable and energise the people in the organisation to find for themselves the hope, optimism, vision and creativity – or any other attributes and aspirations – that they have temporarily loaded onto the leader.

Leaders Speak ...
The short answer is trust. If you trust the people you are asking to make changes in the company, all the changes are surmountable. If you ever lose that trust, the changes become insurmountable. And the reason the team at the top is so important is because that is where trust begins. Are we all signed up to the same goals, values, beliefs and objectives? If that team is unaligned and not signed up to the same goals then any change one is asked to make is unacceptable. And you have to do all that under great public scrutiny – the City, your own people, competitors.

Chairman, luxury retailer

Can leaders escape projection?

Is it inevitable that new leaders will have to deal with this process of projection? To some extent, yes. What supported new leaders to counter the draining effects of projection was to know and be able to articulate clearly the values and beliefs they personally held. Here is what some said:

> *It comes back to one of my very strong beliefs about effectiveness, which is about being true to yourself, being comfortable with who you are.*

> *I've seen too many executives who've got really short fuses. They don't have grace under pressure. It doesn't mean being soft and nice and warm, it means being calm and forthright as to what we are going to do.*

> *I've always gone to companies with products or situations that I feel passionately about. And for me passion is one of the great characteristics of a good leader – I'm pretty driven on that score.*

> *One of the major values I have always wanted to drive has been to show myself as the person I really am. There's no false side to me, there's no very different person at work from the one you will meet at home.*

What these leaders are expressing is their own "north star" – the way in which they navigate themselves through the complexities, demands and ambiguities of transition. In the extracts above are beliefs about personal truth and integrity, about how grace combined with calmness and forthrightness contribute to clarity in times of pressure; about the energising force of passion as a defining emotion of leadership. The conviction of personal values acts as a kind of sea wall against the tide of others' needs and projections. Values enable leaders to hold at bay the possibility of being engulfed by the context of their new role and lessen the chance of knee jerk reactions to people and events. They also help to anchor the individual leader's own internal turbulence during transition by offering a familiar home, a base of personal conviction from which to set out each day.

The clarity of a "values compass" to support the new leader also orientates those around him. Below, a leader describes how important was the loyalty of his team members and how, despite some unpopular decisions he took to restructure his team, he still expected their loyalty to what they were there to deliver:

I think loyalty came into it. I felt after I made these changes that loyalty might have been slipping so I had to have some fairly frank discussions with a couple of my senior team to say "Look, this has happened now and I expect you to embrace the changes. I don't mind having a discussion privately or in the team about what you think we ought to have done but we've done it now." It was establishing that sense of corporate managerial responsibility across the entire team but it probably took me a couple of months to re-impose that and a couple of fairly difficult conversations with a couple of people in managing that bit of the change.

What do leaders do that works?

✓ Know which core values will guide you in this transition and hold on to them.

✓ Be unafraid to voice your values as a way of showing others what you stand for.

✓ Refuse to adopt the role of hero and see it for the trap it is.

Connecting context and leadership: Winning the mandate to lead

If organisations today are complex, turbulent and ambiguous and human beings ideally need conditions of reasonable stability and clarity in order to thrive, how does a new in-post leader balance these two apparently conflicting contexts?

For many of our leaders this question brought them face to face with how they would exercise leadership at a distance. All of them were managing departments and operations which were dispersed geographically, some internationally, and had significant numbers of people (hundreds, even thousands) for whom they were the primary leader. Ways of leading that were available to them in previous roles with narrower scope, were no longer possible; and because, in every case, their mandate was to lead change of some kind, the need to take people with them was paramount. This was more than just a question of communication and getting across information: it took leaders into questions of presence, personal reach and impact.

67

Studs Terkel, in his book *Working*, writes:

[Work] is about a search, too, for daily meaning as well as daily bread, for recognition as well as cash, for astonishment rather than torpor; in short, for a sort of life rather than a Monday through Friday sort of dying.

Although Terkel's book was set in the world of work of 25 years ago, what he says holds good today. There still seems to be a deep hunger in organisations for work to be about more than just the completion of tasks and a wage at the end of the month. In fact, today's organisational and social conditions likely make this need for meaning and purpose even greater. The conditions of uncertainty which can make today's successful organisations into tomorrow's failures: the range of employment practices – sub contracting, outsourcing, job sharing, portfolio roles – which fragment attention and disperse loyalties; and increasingly flatter organisations making for larger roles with increased demands and scope; the need for speed and the complexity of markets, product innovation and delivery of quality; recent demands for corporate transparency and increasingly stringent demands for ethical corporate behaviour. When just some of these combinations of conditions come together, the questions about leaders' reach, impact and presence take on new significance. Leaders don't bring others with them because of their title; nor because they say clearly where their organisation is headed and what its goals are. It seems that people need more than direction, information and targets to commit and engage. The significance of this knowledge for the leaders in our studies was not so much that this is the case, but more the realisation that they were now in the hot seat, and from this place what did it mean for them and how would they need to conduct themselves differently.

How to reach and touch the people?
The head of a large department, dispersed across the UK and parts of Europe, had some fresh insights about himself as a result of feedback he had recently received. He realised, about six months into his new role, that the chances of personally reaching every one of his people (about 4,000) were limited and he would need to think differently about what he "showed" of himself if he was to convey a consistent sense of who he was and how he was trying to lead. The context of his organisation was also significant: it was under regular and demanding public scrutiny whilst at the same time having to bring about rapid and widespread change in structures and practices. The workforce was

largely long serving and, in parts, had entrenched attitudes to how their work should happen:

> *I've got 4,000 people working for me. Some of those people only see me once a year or they read what I say in the in-house magazine. They might see a movie clip of me or something, but they don't actually know me. There are other people who do know me and they say, "Yes, we know Bill, he's alright," but when you're trying to reach out to that kind of a workforce, how important it is for you to show all sides of yourself.*
>
> *Learning about the downsides of an image, whether it's a true or untrue reflection of what the real me is, I thought was very valuable. I could see, "Oh yes, some people could quite easily see me as cold, disinterested in the people and softer issues of the workforce, uncompromising." Whether I am or whether I'm not those things, I could be seen by others as that.*

This leader recognised that people in his organisation would be more likely to give him the right to lead if he was able to show he was more than a one-dimensional man. Given the extent of the changes Bill knew he had to make organisationally, he also had to lead differently. However he personally knew himself, what mattered more was that he was prepared to show to others a person who could respond to the human response that this order of change would produce. Cold, disinterested and uncompromising were unlikely to be the ingredients for building engagement. He had to be able to reflect, in more public ways than he realised at first, a stance towards his people which would be congruent with what they were also experiencing. He goes on to describe the need to show his concern and interest in people and their lives, rather than only their work – and what a change this shift has been for his leadership practice:

> *A member of my staff's father hadn't been well and she had to go back to Jamaica to see him and wasn't sure if he was going to survive or not. She'd been going through quite a bit of pain and I just saw her sitting here the other day. I was rushing around from meeting to meeting as I always am, and I thought, "Should I stop and say anything or not?" I did and was late for my next meeting, but I sat down for ten minutes and I said, "Hey, how are you? How's your father?" All that kind of thing and I think she really appreciated that. She was a little bit surprised that I'd actually stopped and taken time out to enquire. I think that was a big, big step for me in terms of saying "These are the kind of*

69

things you need to do, because if you do these kind of things then people start to see that actually you aren't the unsympathetic uncaring. You have got a softer touchy-feely side, and not only that but you're prepared to share that with them.

It makes people feel more included and more part of the team. I know I could appear to be authoritarian and that some of my team were feeling a bit that decisions are taken and they're not involved. They feel a little bit on the periphery of central policy making and they feel a little bit distant from that. Part of that might be me and the way they see me, so developing bonds with them has now become part of my agenda.

This leader knew that, by changing the impact he had on those he personally met and could "touch," he would influence the impact he had on dozens of the people he could never meet. Moments like these act as stones thrown into the organisational waters. They ripple outwards beyond the reach of any individual, in the form of stories and anecdotes. When those stories embody a response to change that resonates with people in the organisation, the leader's credibility increases and he takes further steps towards building an environment that is conducive to change. At the heart of the mandate to lead are questions about how you make contact with people and how you make connections for people about what is going on that is altering their familiar landscape of work.

Leaders Speak ...

I have spent quite a lot of time reflecting on the question of how to create webs of meaning and what kind of narratives we have. What is the story we tell ourselves about what we're doing and where we're going and how much meaning is there? I have thought about my role as being one of facilitating that meaning as being the single most important thing to do and that has helped me to frame my own job. It seems to me that there's no way I can be on top of everything that is happening here, I have to trust other people to be on top of things and I have to trust that they're going to deliver. My job is to make sure they're all thinking along the same lines so that they all deliver together towards the same direction. The other thing is, I think I have a job to do which is to create a sense of urgency about delivering and the expectation of quality.

Function head, international support agency

For many of the leaders in our studies, connecting with people had brought them face to face with how well they knew themselves and which aspects of themselves they wanted to reveal to others: what is relevant about me without being egotistical? What is significant without being embarrassing? How to be honest without being banal? Only you will know where to "pitch" yourself in your context with the mission you have – and finding that pitch can itself be part of the rewards of this phase. Here is one leader who was prepared to change hugely her own practice when she discovered how satisfying it could be to show her passion as the way to inspire it in others:

I learned a lot about the value of stories to inspire people. I'm not inspirational, but I do need to inspire people through my job. A year ago I was not clear that my job as a leader would be to inspire. Now it's very clear that it's my job. I felt uncomfortable, when you all talked about passion. It felt very alien to me. I don't get wound up. I enjoy my job, but have rarely felt passionate about my job in 28 years – partly because it's not done [where she works]. There's almost a mindset of don't let passion get in the way of objectivity. So I found discussions about passion uncomfortable but this has changed over the summer. I am beginning to feel passionate about my job. It has dawned on me that there are fewer more important jobs than who we employ. It has gone from being just a job to being really important. If you don't let yourself get passionate, how can you expect others to become passionate?

What do leaders do that works?

✓ Take advantage of feedback and act on it to adjust your behaviour to the needs of your context.

✓ Allow yourself to be influenced and "led" by the demands of the transition.

✓ Let go of some preconceived ideas about work and refresh your own mindset.

Expecting surprises: The beacons of transition

The deep dips in confidence expressed by many in the Arriving stage of the role, had mostly disappeared by now and leaders felt their feet were firmly under the table – at least in having a better understanding of what they were in their job to do. Making that happen was the more faltering experience which continued to surprise:

> *The thing that surprises me most is how hard it is to get things done that you want to get done and also – this shouldn't have surprised me – how much of a matrix world we live in. How little you are actually responsible for or how much you have to influence to get people onside. Everyone says "just do it" but if you do just do it then six people tell you why you can't or shouldn't. So despite the theoretical "just do it," the reality is it doesn't work like that: consensus is necessary.*

All new roles throw up surprises – even shocks. These are partly what make transitions hairy, exciting and stressful times. In fact if you accept our view that organisations today are turbulent, complex and ambiguous how could they not be full of surprises? We were curious to find out how self-confident leaders responded to such situations, and how they used these inevitable experiences of the unexpected to support their transition. Were they a source of fresh wisdom? A frustrating waste of time? A threat to their beliefs about control and order? What lies behind our experiences of being surprised is how adaptable we are. How readily we can flex our perspectives, assumptions and behaviour to respond to what is the situation now, right in front of us, rather than the one we had expected or the one we were familiar with last week, last year, in the last role. This adaptability and readiness to learn in the present about the present was central to a new in-post leader's effectiveness and the speed with which that took place. This theme unpicks the inner experiences that dealing with the unexpected gave rise to and the impact of dealing with that for leaders in new roles.

The re-forming of identity

Every transition takes time because we have to adjust and relocate our sense of who we are now in many significant ways. It takes time too because very often we are not consciously aware that we are making these adjustments – or even that there are any to make – until we meet a situation which throws the need back at us. A higher status role involves deciding how to exercise my new power: will I play it like "one of the boys" or hold myself slightly more aloof? It involves working out how important is the "right" title: will I allow myself to enjoy using Senior Vice President? Or leave out the "Senior" so people won't think I'm status conscious? Given a choice of where I sit –

> **Leaders Speak ...**
>
> *For the first time in my career I was waking up in the middle of the night and worrying about the company and the job. I had never done that before. Notwithstanding all the qualities I think I've got, I was being pushed right to the edge and feeling slightly helpless. I think I'd been in the job about six or nine months, and saying it just feels so strange that in my life normally I make things happen positively. It's not that it's all been swimmingly good, but at least, even when it's not going well, I've got a sense that it's going to turn out good. But I was feeling at that moment like I didn't know whether it's going to turn out good or not.*
>
> **CEO, food manufacturer**

literally – in the building, do I go for joining my own team or stay with my peer group? Every action you take – whatever it is – is loaded with questions of identity. Who am I going to be in this role and how will I live out these choices of who to be?

The question suggests that you can choose exactly who you would like to be, but identity doesn't work quite like that. We begin with some inherited traits which come as given, ones we are born with, those aspects of who we are which seem to have always been with us. Other aspects of who we are emerge as a result of our upbringing, the social and national cultures in which we mature and other significant life events. How we combine and use the traits we inherit and the abilities we develop are what constitute our identity. Identity only becomes important, and the urge to adjust it only arises, when you notice incongruities between who you were, who you are now and how you believe your current work requires you to be different.

For all the leaders in our studies their new roles were significant events which at times challenged their sense of personal adequacy and mastery. Several of them went into their roles with clear plans for implementing the brief they had been given, and gave no thought at all to how they themselves might need to change if they were to lead their operations successfully. This realisation didn't come immediately – far from it – for one leader the new role was a welcome change from the personal feelings of failure and stress she had experienced in her previous role, until she began to see that she would need to revise her own attitude to leading if she was to get the satisfaction and achievement she was looking for in her current role.

For another leader the new role began as just a larger extension of what he was already doing:

My predecessor moved on as he wanted a new challenge so I felt my job, coming into it, was really to keep that pot boiling rather than have to go out on my own and rebuild or rejig something. So I suppose knowing the business and knowing the achievements of my predecessor I wasn't as daunted by the challenge as I might have been. I knew I'd be welcomed by the workforce because they knew me. I'd already had a lot of support from people and I think I knew pretty well what I was letting myself in for, and so I was reasonably comfortable and confident that I could do this.

Only months later did he begin to see how some of the controversial decisions he was making would significantly shift his relationship with his team and he would have to find a new perspective on his own leadership:

When you realise that you are the "father of the family" that brings in self-doubt because you haven't got the majority consensus behind you. You're out on your own pretty much because you're the one that's decided to move to this structure and you know they didn't agree with it, but you've done it now and so in a way if it doesn't work it's all your fault, you fool, and why did you not listen to them? So you realise that you're a little bit more on your own. You're the leader and you've got to steer the ship in whichever direction you think is right.

Here Bill is describing the moment when he realised that making the decision none of his team agreed with was isolating for him as a normally highly consensual leader. Standing apart from the team meant he saw himself differently but he also had to be prepared for how others would see him and treat him differently. These are the moments when you act "out of character" to do what you believe is right, and suddenly see a new aspect of "you." Being open to what you do not yet know, being prepared to respond in new ways to what is going on and avoiding the dangerous trap of making the current context into the same as the last one you were leading, these are the ways that surprise fuels adaptability and increases confidence and competence.

Here a leader describes his own search for an appropriate leadership identity, finally settling on the value of consistency and the need to manage closeness and distance as core aspects of how he aspires to lead:

You can't be somebody who loves to be loved by everybody. I was trying to be too much one of the boys. But then I'd yo-yo back into I'm going to be very tough and hard and it was a bit confusing for people. There wasn't a consistency there. One of the kind of catches of leadership is consistency. It's not that you don't change your mind, it's just that there is a pattern and a rhythm. In today's Anglo-Saxon corporate world you've got to make lots of tough decisions all the time whether the company's successful or not. You have some degree of separation but again that then produces a paradox because you can't be too separate from people. So it's finding that line.

What do leaders do that works?

✓ Use new and surprising situations to understand yourself and as opportunities for acting differently.

✓ Reflect on and make sense of your experience as a source of interest rather than self-blame.

✓ Join yourself deeply to the context and to the people in it, by taking the risk to show what and how they were changing.

Resilience and self-belief: The personal fuel of transitions

A common thread that runs through all stories of transition is the experience of a switchback ride: mood swings, days when things go swimmingly followed by frustrating confusion, clarity arriving and then suddenly disappearing, being on top of things and then finding yourself submerged. Whilst this experience is normal, leaders still had to find ways to manage and sustain themselves through such times, without being able to claim any longer the fall back position of being brand new in the role. How are these experiences different from apparently similar ones in Arriving? Confident leaders expect to be on top of any new situation quickly. They apply their experience, intellect and ability to fire on many cylinders at once to their current role and believe it will see them through.

Paint yourself into the picture

The mindset is that a new role is mainly about understanding the business goals, getting to know the organisation and people and then getting on with it. In other words, it is about getting to grips with the external environment around you. The assumption is that, within a few weeks of taking up the role, this environment is knowable and manageable. The simple mistake leaders make is to forget to include themselves in the mix. When new leaders are aware of their own expectations and assumptions about how things will be in the role, and when they have a good understanding of themselves, then when events and situations don't turn out to be as they thought the drain on self-esteem and personal stamina is lessened. Leaders who had the ability to explain events to themselves and others as multi-causal – and include their own behaviour and mindsets as part of the cause – when things did not go as planned, were able to sustain self-belief and maintain considerable resilience.

Here is how a new leader talked about the impact of his own behaviour on getting endorsement from the top of his organisation for a new strategic direction:

> *Everyone is very busy, so the amount of strategic direction you can get is very limited. It's probably my own fault as well, in that I haven't specifically gone out and sought it. I don't know. I think partly it's that this is an agenda which is being driven by an individual at the top of the organisation. And it's probably partly personality as well, I suspect – me as well as them – in that I'm quite happy doing my own thing within the strategic but what you lose from that is this sort of ongoing affirmation that you're going in the right direction, and I think probably I haven't had that.*

These qualities acted as fuel to energise leaders to deliver their agenda as well as supporting them to overcome doubters, resisters and colleagues with similarly high levels of determination and drive. Research into the qualities of resilience have identified the following personal

Leaders Speak ...

I've always known that I've got to have lots of things going on – that's the first thing. They've got to be things that interest me; they've got to be things that are intellectually challenging; and they've got to be things that are moving forward. Those are the four things. If I've got all those four things, and everything else being equal, then I'll have fairly high emotional input, and therefore high energy levels but if they're not all there, then it's the opposite.

Department head, Health & Safety agency

factors as significant: an outgoing temperament, a sense of humour, positive responses to others and the ability to regulate emotions (M. A. Waller, 2001). The Leaders Speak box above would suggest that what also stimulates energy is to be involved in work that is itself intellectually interesting and to have plenty of it. It seems that in the Surviving phase of transition the need for variety, wide range of work and intellectual stimulation – which can be overwhelming ingredients in the Arriving phase – are now the requirements which bring drive and a sense of achievement to a role.

Other factors which leaders described as helping them to maintain resilience were the availability of a set of values (see the section above on the Value of a Personal Compass) that gave meaning to negative or confusing experiences as well as personal support from a range of friends, mentors and former colleagues:

> It is very helpful if you've got somebody who's detached from your business who can give you an external perspective. I've met a guy, a chap much older than me who is a retired ex-chairman of a whole variety of things. And he is very good, he lives in Bristol so I don't see him very much, but he would ring me from time to time as to what his perspective on things was. And you know that was very useful.

Resilience in the face of setbacks and stamina to deliver a punishing agenda all helped leaders to move through the first two phases of transition. But for some, these qualities also helped deal with the more everyday, mundane series of tasks. Here is one leader who speaks perceptively about the experience of leading when the buzz of crises and the adrenaline rush of drama are not present in her work and the leadership task is to be in "the bit in the middle." This is a typical experience of Surviving and contrasts vividly with Arriving when almost every day is a switchback ride:

> Funnily enough it's learning to cope with the stuff in the middle – that's the hardest bit. You can cope with the dramas, I can anyway, it's the bit in the middle where you come in on a Monday and there's no huge dramas, there's stuff to move through, you've got to think about things and it's how you keep yourself and your team going through the bit in the middle. It's probably the hardest leadership task of all.

She goes on to describe how important is the energy rush that ups and downs bring, so much so that she creates them for herself:

Yes, it's that bit that's in the middle that's the scariest bit and it's what you do with the middle bit. I'm always scared I'll lose motivation, be in the middle and say "You know I can't be bothered," so it's that fear that I can't be bothered that forces me into highs and lows. There's still always this kind of unresolved fear that I'll lose motivation, and I know it's illogical because I've been working for 18 years but I feel, am I going to come in on a Tuesday and go "Do I really want to be here?"

The experience of resilience and stamina is qualitatively different in each of these two phases. In Arriving they act like a cruise control to help you drive through the inevitable uncertainty and you need to quickly understand what you are dealing with, to become familiar with how things work in the new role and to get on top of the job so that personal feelings of incompetence and low confidence are reduced as quickly as possible. Descriptions of physical exhaustion, stress and being emotionally drained are common in Arriving: pushing through these and refusing to give in to them are where stamina and the determination to succeed play an important part. Sustaining this kind of push over many months is impossible for most people without exacting a high physical toll.

Fortunately for most leaders, their growing familiarity over time with what their role involves allows them to turn their attention to other facets of managing their transition for which stamina and resilience are still necessary but where they use these capacities differently. In the Surviving phase, stamina is necessary to uphold personal beliefs and values, to support the shifts in self-understanding which any new context throws up and which cause us to rethink who we are and how we operate. In this phase, stamina is more of a current of self-support which enables leaders to stand up and stand out by taking on the personal risks that give them the mandate to lead (see section above).

What do leaders do that works?

✓ Include yourself as part of the cause and effect of organisation change and be open to understanding your role in that.

✓ Find and use appropriate sources of external support to sustain your stamina and resilience.

✓ Be able to operate with highs and lows and manage your energy accordingly.

Thriving: Mining experience and moving on

This final stage of transition is one where leaders really know they are "on top of the job," where they can focus their attention and activity onto the "right" things – because they now know what the "right" things are – and where they know how to make things happen within the specific constraints of their organisation. It is characterised by new perspectives on themselves, their role and organisation. Just getting through activities has been transformed into better insights about what is possible and, for some, a restlessness for the next role.

New perspectives and realisations

The dream and the reality of a job as a senior leader have become integrated as a result of facing into some often harsh experiences and tough personal examination. As leaders looked back on the many months since arriving in the role, they could see they had made significant shifts in their ways of operating; they could identify where their own values and beliefs had been tested and even been compromised at times. They noted with surprise how some beliefs had come to be more foreground than others, as the demands of their unique context provoked them to actively step into what they knew to be right. They could recognise that there were new and unexpected areas of learning for them personally and they saw that the "top" can sometimes carry a personal price which is the sacrifice of intimate personal relationships through divorce or separation. Several could by now see where their own impact had been on their organisation compared with the Arriving phase where they were following through on their predecessor's initiatives.

For some leaders Thriving was a time of mixed enjoyment and satisfaction: the adrenaline rush that came with pitting their wits against the new and unknown had largely gone and without that some leaders saw their role as simply one of maintenance. Some even questioned whether they were significantly contributing now at all. For others, this phase came as a relief from the lurches of confidence and uncertainty they had known when they arrived in the role. They felt now

> **Leaders Speak ...**
> I think I'd underestimated the impact that my behaviour had on others. And therefore I think that would be one lesson that I would give to anybody going into the first senior job is don't underestimate that impact. You might not be seeing people but they are all seeing you. Everybody knows who you are but you don't know who everybody is. I think also to be a person of your word. If you promise something or imply that you are going to do something, it is expected that it will be done and you have to deliver on that. I think those would probably be the key things but my biggest tenet in anything is always be honest, always be honest.
>
> *CEO, Government agency*

they could "wrap their arms around" the job and manage what it contained pretty well most of the time.

The main reflections of leaders at this stage were that satisfying and worthwhile working experiences involved overcoming difficulties, making things different, having a personal impact on events and people, and feeling personally powerful and "in charge." All of these suggest leaders who have high needs for "agency." In other words, to shape and make things happen and to be largely central to the events in which they take part.

Interestingly, Thriving was a time of their role that all the leaders we interviewed found it hardest to discuss. Many felt that the experiences associated with Thriving – significant goals now achieved, recognisable change delivered, new structures in place, and so on – were the signal that their work was done. There was not much more that could be said and it was time to move on. This was a difficult phase of reflection for our leaders. The Western business culture is a fast one. We move quickly past the opportunities we could relish and we seem reluctant to pause long enough in what we enjoy and find satisfying, to unearth what it is about those experiences that cause such enjoyment. A few leaders even acknowledged that they could now see they had initiated new projects in this phase just so they didn't get bored and still felt "useful."

Maybe the old Protestant work ethic is still alive and well after all: keep your head down, work hard and get on with the job is all that matters. We must move swiftly down the to-do list without giving ourselves the briefest of moments to acknowledge the pleasure that comes with successfully completing difficult work. Yet when we do, it can offer one of the simplest ways to unlock new understanding about ourselves, others and the places where we work.

How leaders experienced the final phase of their current role, also affected how they moved into the next one. It was as though the imprint of this role was intensified in the final weeks and months, so that it provided something to be avoided in the next role, or an experience that leaders wanted to replicate.

This leader compares her current role with the one she came from and highlights what she needs to be able to operate successfully:

One of the reasons I'm less stressed here is because I know what I'm here for. In my last role I didn't know what I was supposed to be doing. I had a colleague who I could have worked well with and I'm sure it would have been better if we could have worked closely together, but he wouldn't share anything. I could have added value, but he wouldn't let me. I could have tackled that better, by being honest and talking. At least we could have grown to respect each other's strengths – that's how I've worked before. With this guy, I assumed it would happen, but he never lost his distrust of me. I think he was concerned that I'd try to take the credit for his work.

Operating in that degree of ambiguity is not for me. I know myself better now. For example, I know that I'm better writing stuff than presenting, I'm better when I work with people I know, I'm better with small teams and I'm better when I know what I'm doing. I know now that I'm not a diplomat. In my last job I didn't understand the politics, and what I did understand I didn't like.

Conclusions such as these are typical of the reflections leaders were able to make about themselves and their experience. This leader has now found herself a role which gives her much of what she really needs for success and, of course, which brings new experiences that are still stretching her self-understanding and developing her practice as a leader.

If the Arriving phase is mainly about understanding and absorbing the new context, and Surviving is mainly about recognising what you personally need to change to lead effectively, then Thriving is about making sense of your experiences so you can usefully bring them into service in future roles. Without some kind of reflective questioning about your actions and contributions in this role, you risk just notching up another couple of years of "daily grind." The way in which experience gets translated and absorbed into your leadership practice – maybe even into your life – is by deliberately looking at what has happened to you over the turbulent course of your time in a new role. This is how you extract the most valuable juices from your daily work. So the themes we cover in this final phase all have to do with integrating the significant experiences of a new role into your personal practice as a leader: how the early aspirations of undertaking the role meshed with the reality of what actually happened; how personal life and business success ended up being managed, or not; how leadership became distilled into a few key values and actions; and which mistakes had, with hindsight, been the best teachers. Few of our leaders engaged in regret; pragmatism and moving forward were the driving energies which motivated them rather than looking backwards to dwell on missed or lost opportunities.

Making tradeoffs: Deciding what really, really matters

The early hopes and aspirations that were present at the start of the role have, by now, transformed into other experiences – more mixed and bitter sweet. Leaders with good self-awareness are able to make a fair and accurate assessment of the impact they have in their role, without needing to use false modesty or false praise. They know how they need to behave to maintain their identity and integrity as well as where to be flexible so they can influence. They have learnt what can be changed, what to leave alone and what to be persistent about. They can see through the power plays of colleagues without letting the behaviour of others derail their own intent. They know more about how they operate and play to their strengths. All these realisations help leaders know, from the "inside" of the role, what they must do if they are to make any contribution to their business. Reactivity, on the whole, has given way to responsiveness.

Whilst hindsight makes the past look smoother and easier than it feels at the time, hindsight can also help to bring out the essential "truths" of those experiences. One leader's reflections on this took him into a realisation that working out how he wanted to be personally in the role was as important as what he had to achieve:

> There were times when I felt overwhelmed by the demands on my time, the need to make decisions and the time it takes to persuade and motivate people. No one told me how time-consuming all that would be. I suppose you have to work out in your own way how you are going

to handle all that. A lot of people get on by thriving on business life and they don't want the other people-y stuff. But I do need that and there is a real danger that you just lose that because of what others expect of you. Then you find what you are doing is just not fun – and it should be fun, you should enjoy what you are doing. Here you are running a business, huge responsibility, loads of respect, this should be the pinnacle of your career. For God's sake enjoy it. I didn't initially, but I feel I wasted the first year just having a very hard time.

In the previous section on Surviving we examined the importance of knowing what you stand for and standing up for that. This leader is describing how the cost of forgetting what it was that mattered to him had meant a year of missed enjoyment. The question is, if this possibility had been put to him in the early weeks of his role, would it have made any difference to how he operated? Would he have been able to manage his time better so he did do more of what mattered to him? We can never know. But what we do know from leaders who have been able to take advantage of some of these insights is that a route map of transition does provide perspective and opens up the possibility of choice in how you operate. In the next section of the book we describe how you can use these understandings of your own transition more actively, so that you are exploiting their potential for more immediate gain than having to wait a year – or more – before you can see what might have been different.

The organisational and business context of the role is crucial to deciding what really matters: what will be the focus of the role? Several

Leaders Speak ...
I've got this far by being self-sufficient and the transition from self-sufficient – living and dying by your own decisions – changes when there are more people offering you advice than you need. So being selective of which advice you take becomes really important plus having an awareness of your own biases and strengths and weaknesses. Having a small tight band of people who you can trust to seek advice from as you face landmark decisions is critical. They need to be people who are mature and experienced enough, without too much left to prove – people like this can offer huge nuggets of wisdom.

Group marketing director, retailer

leaders spoke about how easy it is to get diverted from delivering what you are really paid for, forgetting how you can make a difference – although working out what these are can often be the confusion of Arriving and the value of grappling with the Mission pairing. One leader had huge satisfaction from being able to make changes in the flexible working arrangements within her organisation. An issue that she felt passionately about and one which her position allowed her to address quickly. Tensions arose for this leader and others between delivering what they were there for with *how* their organisation's culture went about things:

> *What frustrates me most is the whole matrix management thing. Endlessly dealing with influencers and not being able to just bust through and do it. I have a love/hate relationship with the time it takes to bring people onside and know how important that is with my big motivation, which is just to make a difference quickly.*

What do leaders do that works?

✓ Work out what matters to you personally *and* what the business needs from you. Don't allow yourself to be diverted from either.

✓ Separate what others put in front of you from what you know needs to be done. Go after the latter.

✓ Decide what enjoyment means to you and build it in to your job.

Retaining perspective and finding balance

"How do you hold on to who you are, do what you have to do in your role and still have time for a life outside work?" This was the question – or some form of it – put by many leaders in this phase of their transition. As they grappled with the dilemmas present in balancing all these needs, many leaders were forced to question their own life and work priorities. The questioning for some was brought on by separation from their partner – where their job was often blamed for bringing this about – by increased alcohol consumption, by working through weekends and not seeing children/partners/wider family or by a growing sense of exhaustion when they did stop long enough, such as annual holidays.

For some leaders, a more senior role brought new clashes between home and job which needed them to rethink previous strategies for managing this. Here is the approach one managing director decided on to manage her work and home life. Notice that, paradoxically, to get some balance in her life she has to unload her own hobbies in the interests of her family:

> *One of the big changes in me was that I made some decisions about things I wouldn't do any more. Basically, I cut out everything that is for me. My time is either work time or children time. The starting point is that I put all school events in red and if the children have exams, time to revise with them. I try to have breakfast with them three times a week and to put them to bed two out of five nights in the week. I try not to work weekends other than Sunday nights. That all means I often work to two in the morning because I shift work – I either get up early to work or I go home and put them to bed then work. The net result for me is I don't have hobbies any more.*

None of the leaders we interviewed considered giving up their role or way of working as a result of these experiences, but it did cause them to question how they were working and to try to modify their experience. Several spoke of the value of a partner (usually wife) who could refresh their perspectives with different experiences, or the simplicity that being around their children brought for them.

One leader described how useful his wife was in making sure he didn't "get above himself" once he reached a senior level in his organisation, and how having someone to keep his feet on the ground helped him retain perspective on himself and his work:

> *Jane will never be a corporate wife but she has always tried to support me, go along to events. Equally she doesn't want to get involved in the business like some directors' wives do, but she does have a view and she will say it. Very importantly Jane is my wife not a secretary or an employee of mine, although sometimes if I try and treat her like that she really brings me back down to earth. The last thing you need is that proverbial doormat at home who you can walk all over. For her I am the lad she married when I was 21 and no different – and I have tried to hang on to that.*

The balancing act between home life and work was a source of regret for several leaders – both men and women – and one they rarely felt they had got right. But all the leaders in our interviews were people who had had uninterrupted working lives and careers. This was the realm they had decided would be the place that mattered for them, which didn't mean other areas of their lives were unimportant, but they were all implicitly making statements about the rewards and satisfactions they got from full-time, demanding, senior leadership roles. The question then was how to build in and give adequate, quality attention to other people they shared their lives with. It was noticeable that this question of how to balance different parts of their lives was one the leaders we interviewed moved to spontaneously in our discussions about the Thriving phase of their role. It never surfaced when they spoke about Arriving and Surviving phases. One hypothesis would be that the personal ambition for career advancement coupled with the need to be successful quickly in a role overrules much else – including temporarily, balancing the needs of others in their lives. This is how one leader reflected on her experience of becoming more and more senior:

> *I think if I have any regrets they are not getting the balance in my life right. I was married for 20 years and I wasn't smart enough at realising that the sort of jobs I was doing increasingly as I got more senior would put more pressure in terms of time and stress levels on me as an individual. Looking back, I wasn't smart enough to recognise that and therefore find different mechanisms to deal with things. For the last two or three years that my husband and I were together, we didn't have any live-in help to look after our daughter, so one of us was always under time pressure. And I look back and those are the lessons I didn't learn early enough. It's absolutely OK to spend some of your pay to make your life easier so that you can get quality time with your family. It's just all too easy not to do that.*

What do leaders do that works?

✓ Decide what a good balance between work and home means to you. Stick to it nine times out of ten.

✓ Find practical but doable ways to structure time inside and outside working hours.

✓ Recognise and use as a source of sanity and support people who are not bound up in your work.

3

The tensions
of transition

In this section, we will tackle the principal tensions of transition: that is, the more or less visible dynamics which leaders wrestle with in transition and which determine how things work out. In the second section of this book, we described the leader's inner experience of transition, divided into its three phases. In this section, we will describe the dynamic factors which leaders balance in transition and which determine their actions. What leaders do, obviously shapes the success or otherwise of their transition.

Let us start by laying down some definitions. In their role, all senior managers need to "manage" performance and to "lead" people. Each of these draws on a distinct way of perceiving and thinking.

Managing performance

Managing performance is about finding the best way, often among several options, to achieve a goal or target or activity. There is an enormous range of recurring issues or problems which require this kind of management and which fill the day of a senior manager. To manage performance, the senior manager applies his knowledge about how things work, and often adds in some judgement, to hone down to the *one* best action to lead to a good result.

In the management of performance, problems have a right and a wrong answer, or a better or least bad solution, taking into consideration a range of factors. The answer is either "this" or "that." The choice of one excludes the others. Solving problems by choosing between options is essential to dealing effectively with everyday life. Although there may be many options to consider in performing the management role, the key task of management is to get to the right one. One choice, one preferred option, one best way: the number *"one"* characterises the managing of performance.

Leading people

Is the senior manager thinking in the same way when he leads people?

Experience tells managers that there are no rules or yardsticks for leading people that they can apply to all situations. While managers learn many lessons about leadership through experience, they also know that they must engage with each new transition afresh, with an open mind. They know that if they seek to apply formulae, they will undoubtedly stumble. Reality is too complex for formula to be useful. In uncharted territory, how useful is a map from elsewhere?

We learnt from our research that seeking one best way does not help leaders. We found that successful managers are more likely to hold and balance several factors at the same time, rather than select one and hold fixedly to it. They rebalance these as the context requires, often unaware of any conscious decision-making process. Whereas the unskilled manager selects and identifies himself with one factor, the successful manager identifies himself with many, in different combinations at different times.

The tensions in transition are real and indestructible

We found sixteen factors, grouped into eight "tensions." We have called these dimensions "tensions" because each contains two factors or "poles" which are interrelated and need to be balanced. We observed that these tensions are also indestructible – even if the leader chooses to disregard one of the two poles in a tension, that factor will continue nonetheless to have its impact, only to uncontrolled and usually destructive effect. The only way to manage a tension successfully is to manage both poles simultaneously, consciously or unconsciously.

You will find in the diagram overleaf the name and a brief description of each tension. A subsection will be devoted to each tension in this section.

Tensions are situational

We have learnt through psychological profiling that each leader has a preference for one pole or the other in each of the tensions listed above. This preference is "hard-wired" in him, as the result of traits he was born with. To be effective in transition (and indeed beyond), however, he needs to create an appropriate balance between his preferred pole and his less preferred one, depending on the context. To take the Decision-making Style tension as an example, each manager has a natural leaning towards either more "imposing" or more "facilitating," which he carries through his career. In a given context, should he "impose" or "facilitate"? The answer is that it depends. There is no one right position for the leader, in all contexts.

However, for any given context, there will be a best-fit balance between "imposing" and "facilitating" for each leader. Finding that balance is the leader's job. The more experienced and competent a manager is in leading, the more finding that balance comes naturally

Figure 3 **The 8 Tensions**

1. MISSION: Getting agreement to the extent of change and stability you as leader are charged to deliver.

> To shake things up —— To preserve

2. GOAL ORIENTATION: Being purposeful about results and open to events as these happen.

> To be open to events —— To be intentional about results

3. RELATIONSHIP: Creating the personal bonds with people to give you the credit to lead.

> To develop bonds —— To keep distance

4. RECIPROCITY: Maintaining an acceptable balance sheet of give-and-take between you and your colleagues.

> To seek help, to learn about the organisation —— To give value, by showing how to succeed or avoid failure

5. DECISION-MAKING STYLE: Being consistent but adaptable about when you will lead and when you will follow.

> To impose —— To facilitate

6. PACE OF CHANGE: At every point in time, maintaining the highest sustainable rate of change.

> To go fast to perform —— To go slow to prepare

7. FAITH: Having the best people and structures for the job, and getting the best out of them.

> To clean out —— To develop

8. LOYALTY: Fulfilling the needs of as many constituencies as possible, but without being seen to take sides.

> To support the team —— To serve the hierarchy and/or the wider organisation

to him, without conscious thought. As with other learned capabilities, the leader becomes "unconsciously competent."

Choosing between poles brings downsides

As we have seen above, managers are encouraged to choose between one element and another. With tensions, if one element is privileged to the exclusion of the other, things go wrong. This may take a while, but it almost always does. At a wider organisational level, this is obvious to us. Sometimes organisations decide to centralise (and therefore to stop being decentralised). After a few years, the downsides of that exclusive choice begin to appear. The organisation will tend to become inflexible, and unresponsive to local conditions. What usually happens then? Leaders decide that being centralised is wrong. They switch back to being exclusively decentralised. What happens after a number of years? The downsides of exclusively decentralising begin to appear; strategies lack coherence across the company, people cannot work together easily because of the profusion of different systems. The organisation continues to lurch from side to side without end, consuming enormous resources in the process.

Wanting to choose between centralising and decentralising is the problem. Balancing the two is the solution, according to context. It sounds obvious, but as you will have observed yourself, many organisations lurch from one side to the other on a wide range of issues such as authority versus empowerment, global versus local, or product versus market focus. What we need to do with all complex human and organisational issues is to hold both elements at the same time. We need to find an appropriate balance between the two for a given context. As contexts evolve, we also need adjust this balance appropriately, usually with light touches rather than heavy pulls in one direction or the other.

Experimenting is the name of the game

We have found that this is a new concept for many leaders. Once accepted, leaders find that they need to experiment with balancing before they become skilful. This takes effort and time – and the willingness to take risk. Through practice, leaders can extend the range of ways in which they can act. They can extend beyond their preference and become competent in their less preferred style. With time, they become more flexible in moving from one to the other. This is leadership development in action.

Mission

Many leaders accept unachievable missions. Sometimes, they discover later that the company was not in the state they were told before they accepted the role (as in Sharon's case). In other cases, they accept targets that are over-ambitious (which also turned out also to be the

---

Case study: Part 1

Sharon and a heavy inheritance

In December 2004, Sharon took over as Managing Director of a division of a large multinational in petrochemicals. On the face of it, the business she inherited was in good shape; revenues had been in steady growth over the years and margins were stable. She perceived her mission was to keep things steady and, where possible, develop the business. She had been told by her boss that the contract negotiations with one of the main clients were close to completion and that they presented no problem. As the first months of her transition grew to a close, Sharon came to realise that the negotiations were getting stuck and began to feel these might be symptomatic of a deeper malaise in the business she inherited; this seemed to be confirmed to her when two further clients called to renegotiate contracts. Sharon knew that in these circumstances the division would fail to reach its overall targets and that she would be blamed. Nevertheless, Sharon's immediate boss, David, insisted that Sharon must achieve the planned financial targets. Sharon was in a very uncomfortable position. Should she continue to seek to deliver to the targets come what may, but very sure she would not be successful? Should she resign, accepting that she would eventually be blamed for the mess, and cut her losses early? What else could she do? Great questions to highlight the nature of the Mission dilemma.

---

case with Sharon, given that the company she had inherited was commercially in trouble). Sometimes, leaders accept unclear missions, where they are told little more about their mission than "steady as you go" or "continue to make improvements." As they get further into their role, the lack of clarity in their mission can come back to haunt them, as they do not know where to aim and do not have support for bold action.

Why do managers accept missions like this? A number of different reasons seem to be at play. Firstly, the actual state of the company may not be accurately known to the leader's boss at the time of the appointment. This happens more frequently than one might think – the deeper knowledge of the business, its faults and possibilities, may be held within the business and may even leave with the departure of the predecessor. Sometimes, the boss is disingenuous in his presentation of the business's health to the leader, because he wants the leader to take up the role. This too is more frequent than we (at least) had assumed prior to our research work. Sometimes, the leader feels in debt to his boss for giving him the job and wants to pay him back by delivering outstanding results that will show the boss in a good light. Sometimes, the leader wishes to protect his credibility with his boss by not challenging the boss's description of what an achievable performance would be; alternately he may wish not to appear to be a wimp in his boss's eyes by stating that he cannot achieve a target the boss says is achievable.

Once they are in post, leaders may also lose control of the definition of their mission. In some cases, the leader's boss imposes a tougher mission on the leader once he has taken the job – the goal posts are moved against the best judgement and will of the leader. For many of the reasons above, leaders often find themselves accepting the unachievable.

The mission is the platform on which all else rests. If it is uncertain, wobbly or ambiguous the leader cannot act with confidence or direction. The mission must be got right, in its scope and size, and it must be agreed between the leader, his boss and his colleagues. This work needs doing early in the transition, and revisiting periodically to ensure that it is still the right one. What are the main elements of **Mission**?

1. MISSION: Getting agreement to the extent of change and stability you as leader are charged to deliver.

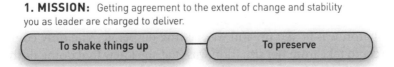

| To shake things up | To preserve |

There are many questions which a leader in transition could employ to get a grip on the reality of his new organisation, but two are pivotal: What should you change? What should you preserve? If you know the answers to these questions, even in general terms, you have the compass bearings you need to set course. Today, more than ever more, the mission of leaders needs to be couched in terms of change; adapting organisations to their fast changing context is key to survival.

When future employers are describing to a new prospective leader the state of the organisation he is taking over and what he is expected to achieve, they are describing their mission. If the description is precise, new leaders will understand what the future employers think the right balance is between the two elements. This balance indicates the strategic intent of the organisation (for example, to be a leader in *xyz* sector) and the will to adapt to changing circumstances. For this description to be helpful to the new leader, it needs to be accurate as well as precise.

Sharon's case illustrates the point. The mission she had been given from the outset was inaccurate, but she did not know that. She accepted the description she had been given about her division and her targets. She had no objective reason to challenge what she was being told. She could not see the invidiousness of the situation she was entering, created by an inaccurately defined mission.

Sharon knows she has to make a move, or she will be blamed.

In fact, her direct line boss David had little understanding of what had happened in the past, and did not feel responsible for it; but because he was held accountable for the performance of Sharon's division's by his CEO Henry, he was insistent that she should reach the agreed targets, whatever their origin. Sharon feared he would interpret any questioning of the targets as backsliding. Sharon was in a very difficult position. She knew her real mission involved more "shaking up" than had been originally foreseen and this would involve lowering the performance targets. She knew that she would need to get her mission changed, or she would be blamed for the current poor performance. She was not sure that she could discuss the appropriateness of the targets with David, without incurring his anger and undermining her credibility with him. To get the mission changed, Sharon knew that she would have to get to Henry; he had been personally involved in the history and had the authority to change the targets. How to get to Henry, but without challenging David's authority?

Sharon was boxed in, and was getting desperate. The only comfort she could take from her situation was that she knew that doing nothing was not an option. She had to take a risk, very early in her transition, to challenge the way her bosses had shaped her mission, and therefore their description of the situation she found on her arrival.

Once Henry (and David, reluctantly) had redefined her targets, Sharon had achieved a more appropriate mission in terms of "shake-up" and "preserve" for her company, in its current situation. She now

Case study: Part 2

Sharon and a heavy inheritance

In March 2005, Sharon came to the view that she could not continue in her role without renegotiating her mission. She believed that this could only be done if she enrolled not only her boss, but also the Chairman, Henry. This is how Sharon describes what she was thinking and what she did:

"I then pulled myself together and I went to see our Chairman, Henry, and kind of got him to acknowledge that there had been deeper underlying issues with the contracts which had not been recognised. Having awareness of the Mission tension forced me to think, 'Well actually, I need to get Henry to agree that all this conundrum with the numbers is due to a reason. It's not that I've come in and I don't know what I'm doing.' Essentially I was telling Henry 'There have been some wrong decisions in the last two years about these contracts.' Because he's been chairman for the last two years, that's a difficult thing to say when you're not terribly sure and you've been doing the job for less than a year or even less ...

"We went to see Henry for the management review and he formally acknowledged that I had been handed a very difficult pack of cards. I just needed someone to say, 'Actually this product wasn't handled very well last year, it's in a bad state, we hadn't perceived how bad, but we want you to sort it out,' and that's all I needed."

Sharon renegotiated her targets successfully, and the platform for her transition was laid more firmly.

had the support to "shake up" appropriately, which gave her the sanction to create new strategy, to lead her division into new products and markets and to employ resources differently. She could now lay to rest her fear that Henry and David were choosing to "preserve" inappropriately, and that she would pay the price for this. Henry had shown integrity by taking responsibility for past errors of judgement, and for his inaccurate description to Sharon of the company's state. Her fear that he would prefer to be complacent or disingenuous was real, but proved unfounded when she provided an effective challenge.

Getting the mission right steadied the ship

After the revision of the targets, Sharon also knew with more assurance what was strong about her company and what should be preserved. She could tell that in the short term she could count on these areas of strength and would not need to use up her energy there. By endorsing these strengths publicly, she knew that she would reinforce her people's self-confidence in a time of change. If Sharon had not done so, she would have been perceived as wanting to change everything (including the strong areas). She ran the risk of communicating that she held "their" company in low respect. They would have concluded that Sharon was lurching too far (from their perspective) towards "shaking up," and they would probably have resisted her. Sharon avoided that pitfall by finding a suitable balance between the two poles, and by explaining her reasons for engaging in "shaking up" very clearly. Her people understood that change was required by the context – not by the ego of the incoming leader. They could see that supporting her to make the changes was in their self-interest and felt affirmed when she endorsed the strengths of the company.

Some principles to bear in mind

1 Take time to understand the specifics of the context the organisation you are taking over is in. Be persistent in getting all the information you want. In general, your inquisitiveness and demand for commercial rationales will be seen as a plus by your future employers, even if it makes them uncomfortable.

2 Before accepting your role, agree with your prospective boss(es) what the context is, as they see it, and what they see your mission as. Clarify what they want you to "shake up" and to "preserve." Get acceptance from them that if the

context turns out to be different than originally thought, then your mission would need to change accordingly.

3 If you believe that the mission you are being asked to undertake is not achievable within the timeframe allowed, state this as early on as possible. Lay your ego aside. Nothing is gained from putting this off.

4 Recognise that your prospective bosses may feel responsible for the current situation, and that they may feel uncomfortable if you question the mission you are given by them.

5 If your prospective bosses resist your attempts to renegotiate your mission, then ask yourself if these are the right bosses for you. They may be unrealistic or asking you to take responsibility for the unachievable. Watch your own possible tendency to engage in heroic leadership.

Goal orientation

The reputation of leaders is determined by the results they have achieved during their tenure. Some of these results appear while the leader was in post; others become apparent after he has left. The truth is that results are more significant than how agreeable people found the leader to work with. Being nice does not rate in comparison to results. Because of this, most leaders wish to achieve impressive results during their tenure. Many of them will go to considerable lengths to get these, because their reputation and self-respect depend on it.

The fly in the ointment is uncertainty. Leaders now inhabit a world suffused by uncertainty; events are unpredictable and planning is difficult. Events get in the way. But being methodical and persevering will not guarantee that the leader gets all the results he wants. These qualities will not suffice. Leaders need to also have the ability to hold uncertainty, to live with it and not to be fazed by it. We call this tension **Goal Orientation**.

2. GOAL ORIENTATION: Being purposeful about results and open to events as these happen.

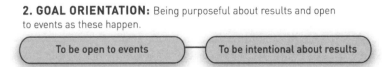

To be open to events — To be intentional about results

Case study: Part 1

Pete's challenge

Pete was newly responsible for a nationwide government service, with several thousand employees. Soon after taking charge, Pete announced that he would keep things as they were, and not make substantial changes in structure.

However, within a couple of months, Pete realised that he needed to change the roles of some of his directors. Two of his regions were coming under intense press scrutiny. He decided to give two directors a regional rather than a national remit, so as to increase the organisation's focus on these two regions which were particularly at risk. Pete was sure this change would be right. He took some soundings with other directors and colleagues about this proposed change, and was told that the two directors would see their change of role as a demotion; they would probably resist and might choose to leave. Pete was worried because they were among his best people.

Pete went to see his boss, and told him what he had decided to do. Would he have his support in this? His boss backed him up. Pete decided to go through with his decision. How would the Directors react? Would he be seen as too changeable? Would he be seen as disloyal? This felt to Pete like a defining moment, early in his transition.

The virtue of being intentional about a result is that it increases the likelihood of achieving it. It focuses our energies, cerebral and emotional, and enables us raise our game to a new level. It allows us to mobilise others too, once they know and become excited about our intent. However, if we are too intentional, and disregard information which suggests that other goals are now more desirable, we do ourselves a disservice. We run the risk of becoming obsessional, and of allowing our ego to drive us, come what may, to achieving our declared aim. As a leader, we sometimes spot the change of circumstances more slowly than our colleagues because we are identified with a goal that we have pointed other people towards. Our personal credibility comes to be identified with a goal we have set.

The virtue of being open to events is that we are adaptable, and able to stay relevant to what our environment expects of us. It keeps us alive

THE TENSIONS OF TRANSITION

Case study: Part 2

Pete wins through

Pete was on tenterhooks for the week after he had met the two directors and told them of his decision. One of them took it particularly badly. He told Pete that his status would be damaged by the change and that he might have difficulty leading his people. The other Director seemed more relaxed about the decision, which almost worried Pete more. He feared he might leave quickly, out of anger.

Weeks went by without Pete hearing anything more from them. From time to time, Pete popped into each of their offices to see what their mood was like. He could not decipher whether they were minded to resist his decision or not. And then months went by, still without any movement.

In July, four months after the decision, Pete took advantage of the half-yearly review to quiz the two directors about their feelings. Both were happy in their new roles. Pete sighed a very big sigh. He knew he had been right to hold firm in his decision to change his mind.

and vibrant, alert to the way life is evolving in its unpredictable ways. It allows us to be inventive, because we are ready to dispose of our accepted ideas and to look afresh. However, too much being open to events can dilute our ability to get things done. If we are forever changing tack, reviewing strategies and being influenced by the slightest straw in the wind, action of any consequence is thwarted. We become indecisive and lack substance, and our credibility suffers again.

Pete's case illustrates the challenges this tension poses to the leader's confidence in his own judgement. When to change one's objective? At what point should one pull away from one orientation and move to another? How to manage the communicating of a change of direction to one's people? What if the decision needs to be taken alone by the leader and he cannot involve others in the change of direction?

Some principles to bear in mind

1 Leadership is inescapably lonely. No one can take away the responsibility that rests on your shoulders. If they do, your job

is at risk. Carrying responsibility involves identifying results you want to achieve. It also involves having your credibility identified with those results. All this comes with the territory.

2   Leadership also means being alert to the context in which your organisation is operating and ensuring you adapt your leadership to meet changes in your specific context. Your credibility depends on you being crystal-clear and accurate about how your context is changing. This also comes with the territory.

3   Knowing when to unlock from a declared objective and advocate a new one calls for judgement. Judgement is subjective, however much data you choose to amass to support your choice. You will not be 100 percent right in all the judgement calls you make as a leader. No leader is. This comes with being human in uncertain times. Don't confuse the business need to change an objective with being indecisive.

4   Trust that you are right in the positions you take, and argue as passionately as you think is appropriate for your case. Make sure the arguments you advance concern the good of the organisation. Beware of your ego's need to be right. If you turn out to have been wrong, do not give yourself too hard a time about it.

Relationship

Leaders derive their power from the followers they have. Followers make an organisation strong because they do the work which produces the products or services that customers value. Followers make an organisation feel like it is moving with energy and with a common sense of purpose. Leaders must create and retain followers if they are to lead.

In what circumstances do people follow a leader? In the first subsection about mission, we described how strongly people need their leaders to set a credible direction for the organisation. For people to follow, they also need to have a strong enough relationship with their leader. They need to feel they know the man who is leading them, as a human being. They need to feel a sense of empathy for his values, things that he holds dear and will fight for.

Case study: Part 1

Dave and his filling out of the leader's role

In early 2005, from being Operations Director, Dave was appointed the Senior Director of the organisation, responsible now for the whole government agency. In one jump, from being "one of the boys," Dave became "the gaffer." The men and women who had been his peers became his subordinates. This is how he describes his experience:

"This was the hardest aspect of my new job. Not only did I need to physically change my behaviour in respect of my colleagues, I also needed to see myself differently. I could no longer be one of them. I could be with them, but not of them, if you see what I mean. As their leader, my position had to be different. Things were my call and could be no one else's. I felt a deep mourning about this change, because camaraderie is so important to me, and I was unused to being alone in this way. They could feel the distance in me that was required by the role. If I walked away from that distance, I might as well walk away from the role, and I was not about to do that. But I had to keep the strong bonds with my colleagues or they would not have worked well with me or done the business. What's more, I actually like a lot of these people. Getting on well with them is one of the things that gives me most satisfaction from work."

Dave applied a new approach, keeping as much friendship as he could in all the relationships. Would he pay a price for this? Yes, he would ...

In addition, people need to feel that the leader knows and understands them, in that he has grasped what they value and hold dear, and will not forsake this. The meeting place between the leader's values and those of his colleagues creates the room for relationship.

Leaders who develop relationship energise their people

In a very large organisation, leaders can personally know only a small percentage of their subordinates. Yet the leader must still find the means to create a relationship with each and every subordinate.

Leaders moving into a senior position need to learn how to create a relationship without being personally known to people. The challenge is to remain personal while using impersonal means of communication, like written messages, video broadcasts and speeches.

When a leader learns to do this well, these subordinates become more present at work, more energised and, in a very practical sense, more intelligent. They act more competently at work. When a leader has created a relationship to his people, and has set a compelling direction, his people can propel an organisation forward to accomplish great goals.

The converse is also true. Without a strong sense of relationship between a leader and his subordinates, great goals are impossible to achieve. Performance cannot be sustained. Motivation cannot be held up. Major difficulties cannot be overcome and new opportunities created.

The foundation of relationship is respect, on both sides. Leaders and their subordinates need to feel respect for the other and from the other. We call this tension **Relationship**; it has two poles, **Developing Bonds** and **Keeping Distance**.

3. RELATIONSHIP: Creating the personal bonds with people to give you the credit to lead.

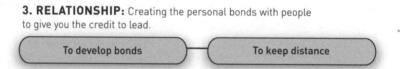

Along with mission, the leader needs to attend to this tension early. These tensions represent cornerstones of the transition process and leaders will find it difficult to succeed if these two are not stable and in an appropriate balance for the context. If the mission tension represents what needs to be changed, the relationship tension represents how work will be done during the leader's tenure. Relationship is a red thread running through the daily operating style of an organisation. Take a moment to notice how things happen in your new organisation. Spot the way three or four typical organisational events take place. For example, note the way meetings are started or ended. Or note the way disagreements between people are handled; or note the people who challenge each other in public. Now ask yourself what kind of relationship between people lies behind the way these events take place. In many organisations, the leader has played a significant role in setting the tone of relationship. In general, the more power, rules and status are used to resolve issues, the less relationships are based on bonds between people.

Over-emphasising one pole creates problems

When we try to change, there is a risk that we over-emphasise one pole over another. When managers over-emphasise Developing Bonds, they tend to lose a focus on the task at hand; they tend to lose their independence from their colleagues and their room for manoeuvre; they tend to get identified with one party or coalition in an organisation. When managers over-emphasise Keeping Distance, on the other hand, they tend to create aloofness and/or mistrust around them; they tend to encounter resistance when they try to get things done; they can also increase the feeling of division within the organisation.

Case study: Part 2

Dave and his filling out of the leader's role

In May 2005, Dave's team was under pressure from both the press and Ministers. Dave received reports that a couple of his senior team were acting in a disloyal fashion, and were "bad-mouthing" him to other departments. Dave checked out the reports and concluded they were true. He decided to modify his relationship to the two individuals sharply:

"I can't tell you how difficult this is proving. I feel that my confidence has been abused by these two. I can now see that I should have kept more distance from them from the start and not applied a blanket approach. They saw my desire for closeness as weakness, and were operating from a different agenda. I should have seen more clearly what was going on. I will adjust this now. I need to understand whether or not these two people can in fact operate in my senior team with a significantly different relationship to the others. We must see how this works."

Dave acted swiftly, but with measure. One of the two directors was removed and accepted early retirement. The second left the Board and took a project role for a year, pending a possible return.

Changing the balance between Developing Bonds and Keeping Distance takes time, and needs to done both towards groups and specific individuals. Dave, for example, needed time to change his relationship with his Board members, who had been his colleagues before being his subordinates. Dave then re-learnt the lesson that he needed to customise the relationship he created to each individual.

Some principles to bear in mind

1   Look at relationships as separate entities, as things which exist, and which can be attended to. (As an exercise, reflect on the relationship you have with each of your senior team. Describe it on paper, perhaps using the journaling/freefall tool in section 5. Consider how you would like it to develop and experiment with ways of making it come about.)

2   Consider the building and maintaining relationship as a key part of your leadership. Remember that leading is always done with others, not to them. To do something with others, relationship is vital.

3   Getting good at handling feelings and people will give you a competitive advantage internally. The more insightful you are with people, the fewer "blind spots" you have, the more you will be sought after for increasingly senior roles. The ceiling most leaders hit which stops their advance is to do with relationships with colleagues.

4   Make it permissible (and indeed rewardable) to talk about relationships at work. The more it is discussable, the more it is manageable!

Reciprocity

Leadership has been described as a social act; it only works if what the leader does makes other people want to follow. We measure different leaders' effectiveness by the impact their leadership has on the way other people act. Normally people do not follow good ideas alone; it depends from whom the idea comes. If the idea comes from a person with whom people have a strong and largely positive connection, then the idea will have more impact. So, we come back to the importance of

Case study: Part 1

Stephen and the new leader position

Stephen took over a department that had lost its way. To its customers, it appeared as a rather typical headquarters function, somewhat arrogant, unhearing and distant from them. The director he replaced had run the top structure without much direction. To outsiders, it seemed like a club of equals – they seemed a closely-knit group, who lunched together every day. The Director acted as their protector and paradoxically also as their servant.

Stephen was given a mission to shake things up, and to open the function up so to serve the organisation's needs. How he related to his top team would determine his ability to make progress with this mission, but he knew this would be challenging. How was he do this if he was largely seen as "bad news"? How could he ever rival the closeness of his predecessor? How could he get enough closeness but also keep his freedom of manoeuvre?

relationship, the theme of the preceding tension.

As researchers, we were not surprised that the relationship tension emerged strongly from the research data and from the many sources from which we have developed our thinking. And yet there was a certain element of surprise for us. We were unprepared for the importance of what one might call "equity" in the relationship, of a sense of fairness in the exchange of give and take between the leader and the people around him, with bosses, peers and subordinates. As we reviewed the data, over and over again, we could not turn away from the fact that leaders needed to *give* to their colleagues in order to *get*, however powerful they might be. Why the surprise? In a way, we were also prey to a myth at the outset of our work which said that leaders are on "send" mode and colleagues are on "receive" mode, and the leader–subordinate relationship is largely one-way traffic. Wrong! It is definitely two-way, and most powerfully during the transitional phase.

Leaders in transition need to face up to not knowing

The great majority of new leaders are at their most vulnerable when they start. Mostly, new leaders do not know much. They may be completely new to the company or organisation, so do not know much about the culture and history; they may be new to the specific business or department they are responsible for, so do not know what makes it tick; they may be new to the function they are responsible for, so truly do not know what people are talking about. All in all, starting out as a leader means that there is an enormous amount to learn, in the sense of acquiring and assimilating new knowledge.

The people around the leader (bosses, peers and subordinates) generally know how much the leader knows or can make pretty accurate guesses. The curriculum vitae tells a story in itself. They also know that the leader cannot acquire the knowledge he needs to lead them (particularly the company and business-specific knowledge) without their help. The leader can either come to them for his education, or miss out. And missing out can carry with it some terrible penalties, because there comes a point beyond which the leader cannot go back to pick up the knowledge. This has to happen early in the transition phase. It is that straightforward. The people in the business (and some outside it) have the knowledge the leader needs. He can only get it from them with their compliance. To achieve compliance, a leader needs to practise give and take.

The **Reciprocity** tension kicks in at the start of transition. Reciprocity means fairness in the giving and taking.

4. RECIPROCITY: Maintaining an acceptable balance sheet of give-and-take between you and your colleagues.

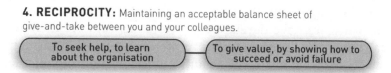

To seek help, to learn about the organisation — To give value, by showing how to succeed or avoid failure

Early on in the transition, the new leader needs to be in high-absorption mode, like a big sponge. She needs to hoover up the information she needs until her head hurts. She needs to live with the fact that for much of this early period, the mass of information she has assembled will only make partial sense, at best. Most probably, the leader will go in and out of a mist, when the information seems to cohere into some kind of meaning, and then blurs again. There will be moments when she thinks "Yes! I've got it! I understand why the people here act as they do," to be followed a few days later by deep despair when she realises "I do not understand the first thing about these people!".

Case study: Part 2

Stephen and the new leader position

He set about building relationship by taking his people's views seriously, and showing that these mattered to him. He also kept distance by making it very clear that he would be his own man when it came to strategy and structure. Stephen speaks:

"I think it worked because of a mixture of listening to them, taking on board the expertise and experience that they had, but at the end of the day making up my own mind that was important. I think the other thing was not coming in from day one saying, 'Okay every boss changes things. We're going to change things and this is what we're going to do: a, b, and c.' I don't think that would have worked. The fact that I was prepared to come in, talk to them and listen to them about their concerns, about what they thought about things, helped enormously, and that helped to bring them along. I think if I had tried to change things without really understanding the business, or them knowing that I didn't understand the business, I think I would have lost them."

He took over a year to get his team ready for the changes he knew were necessary three months in. The team accepted to go where the leader wanted because that direction had become theirs too, in part because of their relationship.

There are ways and means of learning more, faster

There are not many shortcuts that we know to enable the new leader to get through the knowledge acquisition phase more quickly: it takes as long as it takes. The time taken will depend on how new the leader is to the context and how fast he assimilates.

We have observed that the leaders gather more knowledge faster when:

- They go to their colleagues saying: "I am new I need to learn!" Not knowing is not a vice.
- They create a structured process of learning, with a reasoned list of whom they wish to meet and a set of predefined questions.

- They provide their colleague with some value in return for the information and time their colleague has given them. This "give" may be immediate (for example, in the form of assistance from the leader to the colleague to plan or tackle a current issue), or longer term (for example, in the form of recognition of this person's skills and knowledge by involving them in a project or task of value to the organisation).

By engaging with colleagues in an even-handed way, the new leader can learn and build relationship at the same time. There is a virtuous cycle here which the open-minded (and open-hearted) leader can engineer. He can engage with the new system in a way which results in him amassing the knowledge and street-smarts he needs to lead, and the organisation benefiting from the fresh and unprejudiced (well, less subjective, perhaps!) views of the leader.

Fears can create imaginary boundaries

By creating such a virtuous cycle, new leaders somersault the fears that can inhibit each side from opening out. The list below reads rather dramatically. Fears tend to be dramatic, which is why they frighten us off doing things we would otherwise do. Some typical fears of leaders are:

1 "They will think I am a complete airhead."

2 "They are going to ask themselves why I was appointed."

3 "They will take advantage of me."

4 "I will become indebted to people."

5 "I will not know whom to trust."

Some of the organisation's fears are:

1 "He is going to make me feel small."

2 "He will be using this information-gathering to decide whether I am good at my job."

3 "He is going to report back to my boss."

4 "He is going to give me his views, and tell me what to do."

5 "He is just going to take from me and give me nothing back."

To somersault over such a thicket of fears takes some courage and skill. (We describe the particularly expert way in which Laurence did this below.) It requires considerable dexterity to get this tension right.

Focusing on one pole alone shuts down on possibilities

And it is easy to get it wrong by only focussing on one pole or lurching from one to the other. When new leaders overdo it with the "to seek help, to learn about the organisation" pole, they are seen as being lightweight and unsubstantial. People can feel it is "all take" with this leader. People can wonder if the leader is ever going to get around to adding any value, "all he seems interested in is learning stuff!" Too much emphasis on this pole means leaders lose credibility for not having enough to add to the organisation.

When new leaders over-do it with the "to give value, by showing how to succeed," they are typically seen as imposing the solutions a leader used in one of his previous roles. As a consequence, he can be seen as uninterested in the specifics of the organisation they are now in charge of. They can be seen as "not one of us." People can feel disempowered and disregarded, which depresses and irritates them. Too much emphasis on this pole means leaders lose credibility for not having taken enough regard for the organisation.

Principles to bear in mind

1 Most people want their new leader to succeed, and will be willing to help him learn so that he can succeed. Accept their gift.

2 All learning challenges a person's self-image. As a leader, learning will mean that you will have to modify some of your viewpoints and certainties. Check that you are ready for that before you start.

3 Getting a realistic (and holistic) picture of your organisation's starting point requires getting the views of a wide range of people, including some people normally seen as irrelevant or beyond the pale. Ensure that your sample is broad enough to represent the whole "system."

4 Giving value when you know little about the company and its context is a challenge. Work hard to identify valuable things that you can bring early. Make sure that you offer these in a way that others can choose to accept or refuse. Be careful not to impose before you know what the implications are of your decision and are prepared to live with these.

Decision-making Style

Decision making expresses how power is distributed

Power is expressed through decisions. Who decides has power. Who shares in making decisions has power. Who influences decisions has some power too. Who successfully opposes decisions also has power.

Case study: Part 1

Moira and her discovery

In January 2005, Moira took charge of a new merged function combining the HR directorates of two major divisions. This was her first HR posting and she was on the rebound from the bruising experience of having largely failed in her last job. She needed to regain her credibility in her new role or it might become serious for her.

She decided to take charge and let people know who was boss, so she convened a project team to handle the outstanding organisational issues from the merger: structure, systems, product offers, resources and culture. Moira decided to display competence from the outset and took to giving instructions to her colleagues and then holding them to account. At first, this seemed to work, as people appeared to agree with Moira's ideas. As the weeks went by, Moira noticed to her annoyance that deadlines were being missed and people seemed to be passing difficult decisions up to her all the time.

By the third month, it became clear that the project team were demotivated and that the project was unlikely to deliver on time and to budget. What could Moira do? She had already fired all her bullets and whipped the horses as hard as she could.

Deciding who will take decisions and how these will be reached is a fundamental (and early) leadership act in transition. It sets the culture and it fundamentally shapes how the organisation operates.

When deciding this, a leader communicates how he wishes power (and also power's little brother, responsibility) to be distributed. Depending on their personality, and the context, leaders must judge how much power and responsibility they wish to distribute. On the one hand, most leaders know that people take more responsibility when they have power to take decisions about things that matter to them. This argues for wider distribution. On the other, leaders know they are alone responsible for the actions of the whole organisation, and must reconcile the conflicting interests of different parties (owners, customers, employees, stakeholders). This argues for narrower distribution of power and responsibility.

The judgement the leader makes about this distribution of power and responsibility shapes how people engage with their work, and the amount of commitment they have to their organisation. The greater the distribution, the greater the shared commitment (or "ownership" to use modern jargon) is; the lesser the distribution, the lesser the shared commitment is. Each leader needs to decide how important commitment is for the success of their enterprise. In some context, it will be critical, in others less so.

Fear does not work well over time

To pull off the trick of withholding power and responsibility while demanding commitment, leaders generally need to resort to fear. Some leaders choose to do that. Experience suggests to us that fear may work in the very short term, but performance cannot be sustained over the medium or long term through fear. The emotion of fear invariably bring with it behaviours which are unhealthy, such as the unwillingness to contribute, a lack of directness and openness and aggression. In recent years, we have witnessed the gradual decline or implosion of a number of high-profile organisations where leaders employed fear (and rewards!) to maintain commitment. Marks & Spencer under a previous regime and Enron spring to mind.

We call this tension **Decision-making Style**.

Of all the tensions, it is arguably the most familiar and accessible. When pointed out, the tension seems obvious, doesn't it? And yet it is deceptive in its obviousness for two main reasons:

5. DECISION-MAKING STYLE: Being consistent but adaptable about when you will lead and when you will follow.

| To impose | To facilitate |

1   People see themselves as either imposing or facilitating, and find change irksome.

2   It involves both the "how" and the "what."

Let us explain.

People see themselves as fixed as one or the other

Of all the tensions, leaders tend to identify most strongly with one pole or the other. Leaders see themselves as either prone to "imposing," that is, laying down the law, or to "facilitating," (that is, inviting others to help determine the law). Leaders see themselves as either democrats or not. *"I am the way I am, so tough!"* Clear, isn't it? This is a statement of unwillingness to change, which defies the need for the leader to learn and adapt.

Our research has shown that all individuals have a preference for one pole or other of a tension and in this case, to either "impose" or to "facilitate." We have also found that individuals have the ability to develop more competence with the other, less preferred pole. Our problem is that we are usually less practised at using it, because we have learnt to use our preferred pole skilfully as adults. What we are skilled at tends to work; what works tends to get reinforced. These are what we call habits. But in transition new leaders are confronted by more complex situations than they are used to and than their habits are suited for; if they stick rigidly to their habits, as some do, they are less effective in the new position and commonly fail. They need to develop into their less preferred pole which allows greater choice of response because they create for themselves a wider range of options for how they respond.

This issue is difficult, but leaders can successfully tackle it

There are three reasons why leaders avoid developing the other pole of this tension during transition:

Reason No. 1: The issue is not very visible. Leaders do not see the question of Decision-making Style as significant during transition. The problem for the new leader, as he sees it, is getting to grips with the new context, rather than considering the fit between his preferred style and what the context may need.

Reason No. 2: The issue is not discussable. Leaders and their people find this issue difficult to openly discuss, presumably because it raises issues of power and status. These are dangerous and spiky issues, at the best of times; all the more so when we hardly know each other!

Reason No 3: The issue requires skill. Because people have little experience of discussing the issue, they have not developed much skill in handling it. How do you set and manage a discussion about the issue, when everyone has so much at stake?

Case study: Part 2

Moira and her discovery

Moira found that the main problem was her own policy with regard to decision making. It seemed to be fitting neither the context (where she was new and did not really know which way was north) nor her colleagues (who found that they were being asked to take responsibility but had no power to speak of).

Moira decided she needed to work hard at understanding how to facilitate. She used her coach skilfully to identify behaviours she could try out (or experiment with, in our jargon) with her team. In April, she opened the issue out with her team, explaining to them what she had been trying to do and why she now knew it was unworkable. She told them what her boundaries were in any decision-making process (particularly with regard to speed and quality of execution). Then she opened out the question for discussion. Within the space of two (long) meetings, they had thrashed out the difficult issues, and had decided on a new process which met their respective needs.

The team now worked fine. What Moira discovered in the autumn, however, was that she had not covered the same ground with her boss.

Things can get very stuck with this tension, and becoming "unstuck" requires the leader to find another way of dealing with power and responsibility. But to make such a shift during (or even after) transition, a leader needs to acknowledge that choosing between imposing or facilitating will not work (for long). What is required (as with the other tensions, of course) is an appropriate dosage of *both* imposing and facilitating.

Here is one leader talking about his awakening to the need to change his style in this tension:

> *So I learnt that I need to be more explicit than I naturally generally am. I tended to assume that people would pick things up. But it was clear that they hadn't … This is where I think we need to be going to, this is what I think we need to do to get there, based on the discussions that I've had. I think articulating that clearly and openly helped bring them along as well.*

This leader is talking about the need he experienced to shift the terms of engagement with his people if they were going to accept his leadership. He continued talking, now about his two most senior managers and direct reports:

> *I think I've consciously tried to consult and take their views into account when deciding on how to take things forward. I've consciously made an effort to understand their business in terms of the sort of changes they face, and I think to a degree that's helped.*

Decision making involves both the "how" and the "what"

So far in this section, we have talked exclusively about the "how" of decision making, which is the process for taking decisions and the roles of the various players. The leader must set down this "how" and live by it. If it turns out to be unworkable in the context, the leader needs to reckon with that fact. Either change his process or change the context. Normally changing the process is best, particularly during transition. But each leader needs to know where he stands with regard to the "how" of decision making, because the area is full of values. And values are not infinitely changeable. There is a point beyond which each leader needs to take a stand and make clear *"While I am prepared to flex and accommodate, there are some things that I absolutely want to see in our way of taking decisions. From these I will not budge."* Knowing where that point is helps the leader – it helps him be clear on his identity. To this he must remain authentic.

And then there is the area of the "what" – the specific areas where a leader can feel it is legitimate for him to "impose," in any context. While it may be foolhardy to assert that leaders may always "impose" in the areas listed below, our experience tells us that leaders may safely defend their prerogative to "impose" here, if they need to. These areas are:

Values: A leader may (and often should) affirm his values, whatever these may be. If the leader affirms these, however, he needs to stick by them in practice.

Behaviours: This area is closely related to values, but is easier to monitor. A leader may affirm that certain behaviours are positively "in" and others definitely "out." For example, giving straightforward and honest feedback may be "in," whereas bullying and racism may be "out."

Strategic imperatives: A leader needs to set out clearly what the organisation must achieve, the "hill to take," and for what reasons. Massive hikes in revenue or profit pulled out of the air, however, are likely to be resisted unless these are seen as both necessary and possible.

Changes in his senior team: A leader must retain the right to choose his senior team, however unpopular his decisions to change people may be.

For all leaders, the transition phase is tricky because they are in something of a trap. They know that they must communicate some distinctive identity of their own early on. Being bland won't do. And yet, they must be careful what they "impose" early on: they must avoid imposing things which they later state they are sanguine about, or conversely say they are relaxed about things which run counter to some deeply-held beliefs or imperatives. This is an area where new leaders need particular subtlety and judgement.

Principles to bear in mind

1 Most leaders impose values and ways of behaving which reveal how they themselves want to be treated. Other people may have different needs. Check out other's needs early, before setting out your stall too firmly on values, but don't let your needs be trampled on.

2 Decision making is normally a taboo area, which gets a transparency bypass. You will surprise a lot of people by venturing into it with openness and curiosity. Before you do, check what you are not prepared to give up and be clear with yourself and then others.

3 Decision making is rarely included in the balanced scorecard people use. Try installing such a review, with appropriately qualitative metrics, and doing regular reviews with your team. Adapt it to suit, making changes when these become necessary. Make sure the rest of the organisation understands the changes you are making that concern it.

4 Clarifying the decision-making process also needs to take place between the leader and his boss. Start an open discussion with your boss about the area, stating what your needs are and seeing if these can be met. Review the process with your boss when you need to.

Pace of change

Ideally, transitions would not exist, and new leaders would be operational from the word "go." But the phase exists, and cannot be denied. If a leader tries to deny the existence of the transitional phase or to bypass it, he will seriously compromise his chances of success in his role. Not only does the phase exist, but it always takes *time*, whether it is entered into knowingly and with preparation, or not. All parties would like it to take as little time as possible, but there are limits to how fast the phase can be gone through before the wheels begin to fall off the leader's entry into the organisation.

Case study: Part 1

Simon's haste

Simon was a Director responsible for a number of regional offices in Africa and the Middle East from his London office. One of his most pressing tasks was to find a new manager for one of the highest profile offices, Athens, which was under consider pressure at the time as the previous manager had left unexpectedly, with many issues unresolved. These issues were beginning to fester and Simon was starting to get flak from his boss about them. Simon did not know the Athens team particularly well, and weighed up the advantages of appointing someone quickly from London or taking the longer route of involving the Athens office in the recruitment process. Simon also wanted to put someone in whom he knew he could trust to handle these troublesome issues competently.

He decided to appoint one of his deputies, Jean, to the manager post. She was highly regarded and could get to grips very fast with a brief. A week after her departure, Simon was taken aback and even horrified that the Athens staff had cold-shouldered Jean since she arrived. Things were looking even worse, as Jean was getting little cooperation in tacking the thorny issues.

Transitions slow down the organisation's clock

We saw in the reciprocity tension that in transition the leader needs to give value to his colleagues in order to get information from them. It is a two-way street, and a give and take exchange during which the leader trades some vulnerability now for some advantage later. While the leader is learning, he is not fully up and running and there are things which he cannot yet do with confidence and competence. Every time a new leader takes charge, time almost stops, for a while at least. The clock of the organisation needs to slow down to allow the new leader to get on board. And yet, while the leader is being prepared, the pace of the world out there has not relented one little bit. Opportunities are being spawned, problems are being created, business is reshaping itself day by day.

How long will the leader take to be through the Arrival stage of his transition? This will take months. He will not be through Arriving and deep into Surviving within less than six months, in our experience. Should key decisions be put on hold while the new leader is learning? Some just cannot be. At what point will he be able to take decisions himself? This cannot come soon enough. While he is not yet able to do this, how should decisions be taken and who should take these? This needs to be decided! Is the new leader responsible for such decisions? Of course he is.

These are some of the questions which cannot be shirked early in transition. Exceptionally, the new leader will join at a time of relative peace and quiet for the business. His boss will be relaxed and keen for him to get his bearings in good time. He will be spared the need to endorse significant decisions early. He will have the time to work himself into his role in a measured and gradual way. He may even have

Case study: Part 2

Simon's haste

Two months in, and Jean was hanging on to her Athens position with determination, but still without local support.

Simon decided to act. He invited Jean and the top seven executives to meet him in nearby Rhodes for a two-day meeting break. Simon decided to lance the boil at the opening of the meeting. He told the group the story of Jean's appointment, his reasons for moving fast and his feelings of worry since she had landed in Athens. Five of the Athens executives spoke next, each telling their story of the departure of the previous manager, and of the serious organisational problems which he had not attended to. Simon realised that in his haste to deal with the thorny issues he had skimmed over the deeper crisis in the office. Jean's appointment without consultation had confirmed the seven executives in their view that London was out of touch. They told Jean that they had decided to freeze her out, to send that message to London.

So began the long march back from the brink. Slowly, relations repaired. Eight months later Jean returned to London, and one of the seven executives was appointed manager. Simon reflected on the costs his haste had involved.

been appointed to bring new life into a sleepy business, and may have plenty of time to prepare his moves. Lucky man! But dreamers beware! This situation is not the norm today.

Today time is short

The far more likely case today is that the new leader will join a train which is moving at a considerable pace, and where major decisions from the new leader are eagerly awaited. Not infrequently, these decisions have been held over by colleagues until the arrival of the new leader, and they will expect that these to be taken now, without any more delay.

Not infrequently, the new leader's predecessor will have been moved on or out, leaving a major leadership vacuum for months. The new leader will probably be expected to instil a mood of urgency and to intervene rapidly to set things to right. In such circumstances, the pressure to cut short the grace period of the new leader will be strong.

On other occasions, the new leader will join at a time of major upheaval of the business (rather like Sharon's case in the Mission tension), and immediately will be handed the controls by her boss and told to "sort it!" The boss will argue, with good cause, that customers are neither interested in nor mollified by their supplier's internal transitions. Difficult!

The most usual situation today is that the new leader will find that his boss puts pressure on him to achieve major objectives quickly; this pressure may be exerted implicitly, without explicit deadlines, but it is almost always there, in fact. The alert new leader will make his mind up about what his boss' real expectations of him are – these are never less than what the boss states, and are almost always greater!

By calling this tension **Pace of Change**, we wish to communicate the pressure on the leader to get going as fast as he can, but without the wheels falling off.

6. PACE OF CHANGE: At every point in time, maintaining the highest sustainable rate of change.

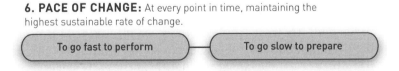

One pole (to slow down to prepare) represents the pressure on the leader to slow the clock down, to enable him to get fully on board. The other pole (to go fast to perform) represents the pressure to hit the ground running without any delay whatsoever.

The risks of going too slow can be that people will lose confidence in the leader because they perceive him as oblivious to the urgency of the situation confronting the company. Being seen as unconcerned on the bridge never helped a leader. Also, the leader may fail to make some key decisions in time, with major implications for the future of the business.

The risks of going too fast are that the leader goes in above his head and makes hasty decisions, which have negative implications further down the line. Leaders cannot take major decisions about structure or strategy without a real grasp of how the business works. Through doing too much early on, the leader may also run the risk of losing credibility with his people, because they see him acting as something of a headless chicken. Being highly active early on can come across as panic-stricken.

So leaders need to get the dosage right between doing the urgent things that absolutely need to be done and taking the time to learn enough to be able to take good decisions.

Some principles to bear in mind

1   Leaders get on top of different areas at different speeds, and need to know when they are ready to move confidently to make decisions.

2   If you really do not know "which way is North," make this clear as transparently as you can. It usually pays off to state this publicly. Not knowing what to do, and acknowledging this, is a "leadership act." People respect humility in a new leader; although they may be initially discontented by a lack of urgent action, they invariably condemn a leader judged to have taken decisions in a hasty and thoughtless manner.

3   Early on a leader cannot rely on his senior team to take decisions on his behalf – the leader does not yet know whose judgement to trust, professionally or ethically. The bond between him and his colleagues is also fragile at this point. Be mindful not to delegate power lightly at the early stage.

4   Like most groups, the senior team will contain differences of vision and approach. The leader will not be able to detect these with accuracy early on. Be careful not to fall into the trap

of siding with one personality or faction in the team. Preserve your autonomy, while building bridges with everyone.

5 The mission should answer two questions for the leader: how high does the boss expect us to jump? And by when does he expect us to do this? Make sure that you have agreed the answer to the latter question, and that full allowance has been made for the time your transition will take. If in doubt, return to the principles of the mission tension for guidance about negotiating mission.

Faith

By appointing the leader, the bosses of the organisation have expressed their faith that the leader will be up to the job. They have expressed their conviction that he is the best available man for the job and that he brings the capability and experience required to be successful. They know that in most cases he will need to undergo an intense learning period about the organisation he is taking charge of. However, they are confident that he will be able to do that in good time. They believe that he will overcome the developmental challenges in front of him.

By appointing a new leader, the bosses have also put some of their credibility on the line with the people of the organisation: if the leader does not prove up to the job, their judgement will be impugned. If these bosses prove repeatedly unable to find effective leaders for the organisation, they may be replaced themselves. Similarly, one of the prime qualities the bosses require of a new leader is the ability to know what (and whom) needs changing, and by when. The flip side of that same quality is the ability to know what (and whom) can be developed and is worth retaining. We call this quality "faith."

Are these the toughest questions for leaders?

Immediately on taking charge, the new leader will need to ask himself over and over again: do I have faith that this person has it in them to be successful in my organisation? Do I have faith that this team has it in them to be successful? Do I have faith that this element of organisation (ie structure, procedure, system, process) is good enough for the job? Few leaders assume that everything and everyone that they have inherited will be right for the challenges ahead.

The dilemma that confronts new leaders is this: should he invest time and money in a person or element of organisation, in the hope of

Case study: Part 1

Julian and the unsettled team

Julian was appointed by the senior Director to oversee and manage the existing Operations team, which his boss had managed up to that point. The three directors in the team were experienced and successful. They knew the business and had played a major role in creating the organisation as it was. Julian decided to spend his first few months getting to know the detail of each of their businesses, so that he knew what they were talking about and could assess their progress. At first, his information-gathering was welcomed by the directors. But as time wore on, and as Julian began to give instructions to some of his directors' direct reports, some tensions grew up in the team. Julian was worried because one of his three directors was clearly overwhelmed by the demands of her job, and was beginning to lash out at her subordinates. Did he know enough though to move her on? How would he fill her very demanding role so early in his tenure? Julian did not know what to do .

successful development? Or should he change them? The new leader knows that the time he has to be successful in his role is necessarily limited. Even if this limit has not been defined by his boss (it most likely has not), it will be there all the same. The leader is therefore embarked on a real race against time to be successful. This success will only be possible if he has the right people and organisation in place and if these have been working long enough to fire on all four cylinders. The leader knows that beyond a certain point in time it will be too late to make changes which will have the desired impact before his time limit is up. So the leader needs to act as early as possible to make changes, and yet early on the leader is usually not well prepared to make such decisions.

The leader is confronted with this dilemma most immediately with regard to his top team. New leaders need to establish their top team as soon as possible. Getting a loyal, competent and aligned top team is essential to creating a stable platform for the leader. To get this team, the new leader may well have to change (or to "clean out") some of its members, whom he judges to be wrongly or inadequately skilled for their role. Other members the leader may judge to be below the level required, but he may have faith that they can fill out (or "develop" into) their roles, within an acceptable timeframe.

This is the **Faith** tension.

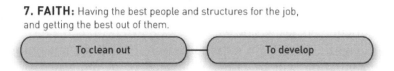

7. FAITH: Having the best people and structures for the job, and getting the best out of them.

| To clean out | To develop |

When tackling the composition of his top team, the conscious leader will feel the tension of the Pace of Change tension (go slow to prepare/go fast to perform) acutely at this point. He needs to remove and acquire team members as fast as possible, preferably within the first few months. But he also needs to make extremely good judgements about senior people, as he may be gravely compromised if he either disposes of uniquely valuable people or acquires unsuitable people. The implications of poor decisions will live with the leader throughout his tenure. Leaders often talk of intense feelings of loneliness. Few decisions are lonelier than the selection of the top team.

The views of leaders we work with tend to support "surgical" intervention by the leader with regard to the senior team in their

Case study: Part 2

Julian and the unsettled team

Julian decided to play a long game, and not to replace the struggling Director. He was concerned that raising the issue of her performance would unsettle the small team and that the turbulence would undermine his directorate's credibility. One year on, the struggling director was still in post. The other two directors had begun to question Julian's leadership capability and challenged his right to continue to bypass them. Julian was wondering whether he should have acted earlier.

organisation. Once the leader has established his top team, he is freer to adopt a variety of "faith" styles, dependent on the context and his particular style. The way a leader holds the faith tension has a major impact on the culture of an organisation, because it determines who is "in" and who is "out" and how exits and continued membership are managed. The manner in which a leader exits people is highly significant. While there may be a case for exceptions for people who are being disciplined, leaders do well to always exit people in a respectful and thoughtful way. If for no other reason, the people remaining in the organisation will be either motivated or de-motivated by the leader's style in this area.

Some leaders intentionally use the exiting process to foster a strong feeling of belonging in their organisation, because they want a prolonged commitment from their people. Such commitment may, depending on the sector, be important for sustained performance. Other leaders create organisations with a more "easy come, easy go" feeling about them, because they believe that their organisation will achieve higher levels of performance by being able to change people more flexibly. In both cases, treating exiting employees well makes abundant sense.

Choose to balance the two poles

The leader shapes the culture of the organisation by how prepared she is to "clean out" and to "develop." Her behaviour here will probably be influenced by the balance of the Mission tension, where the mix of "shake up" and "preserve" has been decided. Leaders need to find the appropriate mix for their organisation between "cleaning out" and "developing." The solution is not to choose between the two but to combine them effectively for the circumstances. There are clear downsides to making a choice, between "cleaning out" or "developing." If a leader chooses to exclusively "clean out," then he can be confident that he will gain a reputation for disparaging the people in the organisation he has taken over. They are likely to both resist the leader and to lose confidence in themselves. They will see the focus of the business as short term, and their future within it as well.

If a leader chooses to exclusively "develop," on the other hand, the leader will come to be seen as overly protective and to lack the courage to take necessary, hard decisions about people blocking progress. Because of the absence of new blood, people will perceive that the organisation is becoming too in-bred and inwardly focussed, and will fear for its future.

Some organisations where the culture has become very cosy may actually do little "cleaning out" or "developing," and may enter a negative spiral of under-performance.

The leaders of organisations bear a clear and unique responsibility for ensuring that the faith tension is being held healthily. They cannot delegate oversight and strategic direction for this area to the human resources department. They will partly shape how well connected their organisation is to the market and society at large by how firmly and appropriately they hold the "faith" tension.

Some principles to bear in mind

1 Early in transition, the policy a new leader communicates through words or actions to either "clean out" or "develop" is monitored very closely by the people in the organisation. They will often reassess their own future in the light of the policy they perceive. Be very careful that you are in control of the message you are communicating.

2 How a leader gets rid of people is almost as important as whom he chooses to get rid of. Be mindful of the fact that people are often intensely loyal to their colleagues and will want them to be well treated if they are to be removed. They will also want the terms of separation to be "human," because they fear they too may experience separation.

3 The way an organisation develops people communicates how it believes people learn and how open it is to new ideas. The more challenging and controversial the way, the more people will perceive that the leader wants to keep the organisation in touch with external developments. As the leader, make sure you are involved in the shaping of the way development is done.

4 Bringing in new blood to an organisation facilitates change. Knowing how much new blood to bring in, and at what pace, is a matter of important judgement. The greater the influx, particularly at senior levels, the greater the need to apply counter-balancing effort to maintain stability. Remember that the time it takes to build new relationships is much longer than the time it takes to gain knowledge or to agree

new processes. Work hard to ensure the relationships throughout your organisation are strong and collegiate.

5 The leadership group of an organisation is the weather vane of both change and stability. How this group changes shapes much below. Be particularly attentive as the leader of the whole organisation to ensuring that your intentions for the future are clearly and regularly communicated.

Loyalty

In organisations, all leaders are in an "in between" position. They are at the junction between the hierarchy above them and their organisation below. Although this position brings difficulties with it, it defines leadership and cannot be avoided.

Leaders have bosses in the line or on the Board. These people have appointed the leaders and are responsible for their performance. Leaders answer to these people and need to fulfil their expectations as best they can. These bosses need to feel that the leaders are fighting their corner and are defending the interests they (the bosses) represent. In response for these actions by leaders, their bosses will support them to succeed in their current (and possibly future) roles. Leaders need to feel that their bosses will fight their corner when the going gets tough. That support is essential to leaders' confidence, as we have seen in the Mission tension. That is one side of the story for leaders.

Leaders also have subordinates who answer to them, and who must act to realise the direction the leaders have set out to follow. Without the active support of these subordinates, the leader's direction cannot be achieved. Leaders need to feel that their subordinates are fighting the corner of this direction, and are committed to the purpose of their organisation. As we saw with the Decision-making tension, leaders stimulate and reward this commitment in their subordinates by distributing power and responsibility to them. Leaders are valued by their subordinates in part for their ability to make it easier for them (the subordinates) to be effective in realising their sense of commitment. Subordinates also expect their leaders to fight their corner against pressures from above the leader or from other parts of the organisation. In response for these actions by the leader, subordinates will support the leader when the going gets tough. That is the other side of the story for leaders.

Case study

Rupert's loyalty dilemmas – A typical story

Rupert was brought in from the outside as COO of one division of a global energy company. He was new to the sector and to the company. To start with, he did not know the ropes of anything much. He was ambitious to prove himself and to move into even bigger roles before long. Rupert's MD, a protégé of the group CEO, was fast-moving and driven by the achievement of short-term goals. Rupert decided to attempt to meet his MD's demands for short-term performance, while also pursuing medium-term objectives which the MD did not think were important.

After four months in the role, Rupert increasingly found himself at odds with his MD, who instructed him to let go of the medium-term work. Rupert was disgruntled and down-hearted. Had the Chairman of the company not called on senior managers to focus on the medium term as a priority?

Shortly afterwards, the chairman fired the CEO and replaced him with a new man who nailed his colours to the mast: build strength for the medium term! One of the new CEO's closest advisers approached Rupert and told him that he was being looked on favourably by the new CEO. He might be offered a new role.

Rupert's MD made contact in the following days and advised him to stay loyal to him in turbulent times. Rupert was torn between two loyalties: one to his boss and to his own team, and one to the new hierarchy and to his rapidly ascending career.

For leadership to be possible, all of these expectations need to be working at the same time. The leaders' bosses and their subordinates need to feel the leader is fighting their corner, which leaders need to do. The leaders also need to feel that their bosses and subordinates are fighting their corner too, which they need to do. Leaders are at the centre of this web of expectations, and by their actions largely determine whether or not this web breaks or holds together. They are truly in an "in between" position, between groups which at times hold conflicting interests and visions. In this situation, the "in between" position of the leader can be enormously difficult to hold.

8. LOYALTY: Fulfilling the needs of as many constituencies as possible, but without being seen to take sides.

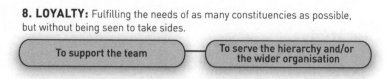

To support the team — To serve the hierarchy and/or the wider organisation

We call this the Loyalty tension.

As we have seen with the other six tensions, leaders cannot decide to choose between one pole or the other. They must hold both poles at the same time, with varying emphasis depending on the context. But they must never let their grasp of either pole go entirely. In some cultures and with some bosses strong expectations are created about which way the leader should lean that it can be very hard to hold both simultaneously. So when this is the case the skill of the leader is to act counter culturally without alienating those whom he also relies on for his support. This is a classic "between a rock and a hard place" scenario.

If leaders choose (or allow themselves to be seen as having chosen) to exclusively serve their bosses, they will be seen eventually (by their subordinates) as having become "the boss's men." They will become isolated from their staff, who will become gradually less responsive to them. If they choose (or allow themselves to be seen as having chosen) to exclusively serve their subordinates, they will be seen (by their bosses) as having "gone native." The leaders will find that their bosses challenge them more forcefully and support them only sparingly. They will feel isolated again.

When leaders manage to hold both poles at the same time, they give themselves the opportunity to succeed, even in extremely trying circumstances.

Some principles to bear in mind:

1   As a leader is in an "in between" position in an organisational system, what he does in respect of one part of the system affects some or all the other parts. As you consider each action you intend to take, think about how it will be seen by each part and what its impact on them will be.

2   When different parties in an organisation (for example, a leader's boss and his subordinates) hold conflicting interests and positions, the leader should ensure that these parties are aware of each other's interests and positions, unless confidentiality prevents this. The objective is more than transparency,

and is a valuable goal in itself; it is to spread information about what different parties see as important.

3 The leader's boss may seek to impose objectives that the leader disagrees with in some respect or another. The leader may challenge these objectives with his boss, and may be unsuccessful. In these circumstances, the leader is confronted with questions about his relationship to his boss. What is the meaning of this imposition? How effective does the boss think the leader can be in such circumstances? Leaders must avoid the temptation to create triangles, using their people to help undermine a remit from above they disagree with.

4 Both the leader's boss and his subordinates know that the leader is in an "in between" position, sometimes a very difficult one. This fact is not a secret. When the organisation is managed well, and the relationships between parties are respectful, all parties know that the leader cannot please them completely at all times. You can't please all the people all the time! The view that you can is patently unrealistic but people may still hold it.

What's priority in transition?

When as leader you arrive in your new office on the first day, you become aware that you have oceans to learn, and that there are a ton of things that you could start doing. It can be tempting to try to get to grips with everything, without discrimination. Yet you know that you need some way of sorting out what really must have your attention from that which can wait or be given to someone else. You assume that what was important in your last role may not be so in this one. You know it will take time to develop a sense of what is really significant in the new context, but you have to deal with strong pressures on you (from above, from below and from inside!) to get active early. What criteria should you use to make such a selection? You assume that there must be things that all leaders in transition need to attend to, but which ones are they?

To find answers to these questions, we look to the fundamental accountabilities of leaders. What are these? If they do nothing else, leaders need to ensure that their organisation has enough of the following elements, and of the right quality:

- Direction: Which way do we need to go?
- Organisation: How should we distribute and orientate our resources?
- Relationship: How should we behave?
- Leadership: What do we stand for?

In transition, leaders need to grip these accountabilities with special vigour. They need to get a handle quickly and accurately on what the current position is with each, and to decide which of these requires priority action over the next six to nine months. In transition, we call these accountabilities the "core areas." There may be specific issues outside these "core areas" which you need to deal with urgently in your new context (for example, the court case or insurance claim that cannot wait). But, as a rule, you will find your priorities in one of the four core areas, which we describe below.

1 **Agreeing business objectives.** You need to know what performance difference your organisation is expected to make, however performance is defined. You need to know by when this difference needs to be made. And you need to agree with your boss(es) and your people that these are achievable and motivating. In some cases, you may need to work with your boss(es) to create a better definition of those business objectives. Business objectives are what your organisation produces, be that a product or a service, or both. (Mission as described above covers both business objectives and organisational objectives, which are covered in the three core areas below.) Hazy or wrong objectives spell trouble down the line.

2 **Organisational structure.** You need to know if your organisation needs changing, in some of its "hard-wiring." By this we mean how resources are allocated, how these are bunched into structures, or what processes and systems are essential to have. Poor structures reduce capability, sometimes critically.

3 **Asserting culture.** You need to know if your people hold the right values and beliefs for the job of the organisation, and whether they behave in ways which maximise the use of the organisation's physical, financial and intellectual resources. Are people pulling together? Are they pulling in the right direction? Culture can be the silent killer, or the great advantage.

For the purposes of clarity, the kinds of cultural changes a leader may wish to introduce include items such as:

- Encouraging people to take more risks.
- Developing more knowledge of and interest in customers.
- Making managers less authoritarian.
- Making managers more decisive.
- Taking more care about people's development.

4 **What leaders stand for.** As leader, you need to put yourself in the "right place" for you to be effective, in relation to the many competing groups of people vying for your support. You need to know whom you (and the other leaders) exist to serve: the wider corporation? The Board above you? Your boss(es)? Your own division or subsidiary? Other divisions or subsidiaries? Your people? Yourself? Is the answer "all of the above"? If so, how will you make decisions when you are torn between loyalties? A leader without loyalty lacks passion; a leader with too much loyalty lacks freedom.

Again, for the purposes of clarity, the kinds of positions leaders may choose to defend include:

- The importance of respecting hierarchy.
- The need of people throughout the organisation to be heard.
- The case their organisation wants to passionately make to the Board.
- The equity of "give and take" between people, whatever their status.
- The importance of the survival of the organisation.

Will there also be matters of detail which await you on your arrival and which demand your attention? Yes, because these matters are irritating (or energising) people, and because they want you to attend to them straight away. Should you deal with them early? Probably not, and for a couple of reasons.

The first is that you need to stay "big picture" at the start. The risk of getting lost in the trees is real. Dive into detail from time to time (if you must), but swim back to the surface quickly, and take as few early decisions as possible. There are crisis transitions where this rule cannot be obeyed – we know that. But these are exceptions. The second reason is that issues of detail are almost always connected to issues of signifi-cance (like power, or distribution of resources or conflicts between people). If you make decisions on issues of detail, you can rarely avoid being seen as "taking sides." The problem is not with taking sides, as such. The problem is taking sides when you do not know that you are doing this, or on whose side you are now seen to be. A leader can lose precious credibility by sorting out detailed issues before he knows what's really going on.

You cannot know which of the core areas is going to require your attention first of all. It will depend on the context you are in. The context will determine which of the "core areas" you need to attend to first in your transition. There is no sequence to follow, like: start with sorting strategy, then move to sorting resources, then improve the processes .... You could waste a lot of precious time following a sequence shaped by someone else. You need to find out for yourself what the context requires. You should gather the data, and make sense of it. You will make your leadership by doing this well. In section 5, we provide you with two tools to help you to identify the core areas which can direct your attention in transition and beyond.

In our introduction to section 3 on tensions, we made the point that how leaders "hold" the tensions has a determining impact on the success of their transition. The reason why this is true is that the ten-sions emerge directly from the importance the core areas have for the leader. The tensions are what leaders and other people feel (and need to balance) when they are trying to reconcile a core area with reality. In practice, each of the tensions is particularly relevant to one of the core areas; it is as if that tension illustrates most powerfully what is at issue, when push comes to a shove, within the core area.

Agreeing business objectives

For example, when it comes to the business objectives, these questions matter most during transition:

- How much change do we need to make, and why? How will we know if we have successfully done this? (Mission)
- What needs to be maintained in our performance? What threats to our current position do we need to protect against? (Mission)
- How correct are our existing goals and targets? Why are they worth maintaining, or changing? (Goal Orientation)
- How can we stay alert and able to flex our goals and targets according to the evolving situation? (Goal Orientation)

Organisational structure
These are the questions that are most pertinent for structure, under-stood as the "hardwiring" of the organisation:

- How roadworthy are each of my key people, the main struc-tures, systems and processes in my organisation? Do I need to radically change any of them? (Faith)
- What can be done to get the most out of the potential of our people, structures, processes and systems? (Faith)
- How urgent is it to act so as to keep up performance? What pressures should not be resisted? (Pace of Change)
- How much time is needed to prepare the big decisions and steps that are needed? (Pace of Change)

Asserting culture
In this core area, which is notoriously challenging for new leaders in-post, here are the typical questions which are pertinent:

- How much distance do I need to keep from my colleagues (boss and subordinates) to maintain my authority, my room for manoeuvre and my clarity of thought? (Relationship)
- How much trust and warmth should I create with my col-leagues, so that I can benefit from their support and goodwill? (Relationship)
- How much should I involve others in deciding our strategy and everyday planning? How much power do they need to have to be committed? (Decision-making Style)
- How much should I lay down what I think should happen, setting direction firmly and authoritatively? (Decision-making style)

What leaders stand for
In this core area, which speaks to the leader's position relative to other people and to important issues, the key questions tend to be:

- How much should I jump in and give people the benefit of what I know and think? (Reciprocity)
- How much should I lean on my people to help me to learn about the organisation and its business? (Reciprocity)
- How much should I support the needs of the hierarchy above me and the needs of the wider organisation? (Loyalty)

- How much should I support the needs of the team I am part of? (Loyalty)

The 8 Tensions distribute as follows across the four core areas.

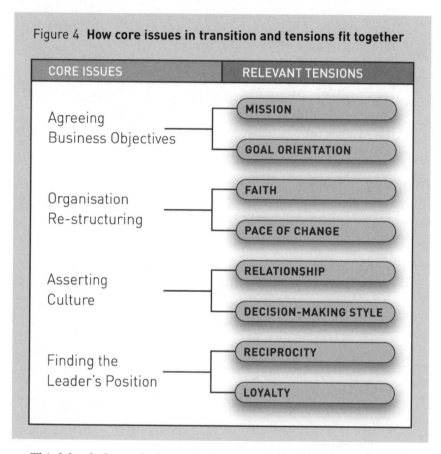

Figure 4 **How core issues in transition and tensions fit together**

CORE ISSUES	RELEVANT TENSIONS
Agreeing Business Objectives	MISSION
	GOAL ORIENTATION
Organisation Re-structuring	FAITH
	PACE OF CHANGE
Asserting Culture	RELATIONSHIP
	DECISION-MAKING STYLE
Finding the Leader's Position	RECIPROCITY
	LOYALTY

Think back through the transitions you have known, and ask yourself how the tensions described in this book applied to the core areas that were relevant in your case. Not all the tensions will be highly relevant at the same time in your transition. Normally, we find that three to four tensions have a special power during each leader's transition; how he manages these will either slow him down or enable him to get his feet under the table faster. How he manages these also reveal how well the leader possesses some inner qualities, which are critical to successfully navigating his way through transition.

Of the four "core issues," business objectives are the most easily measurable – they are the most visible of the areas. "We either hit our

Figure 5 **The worlds of transition**

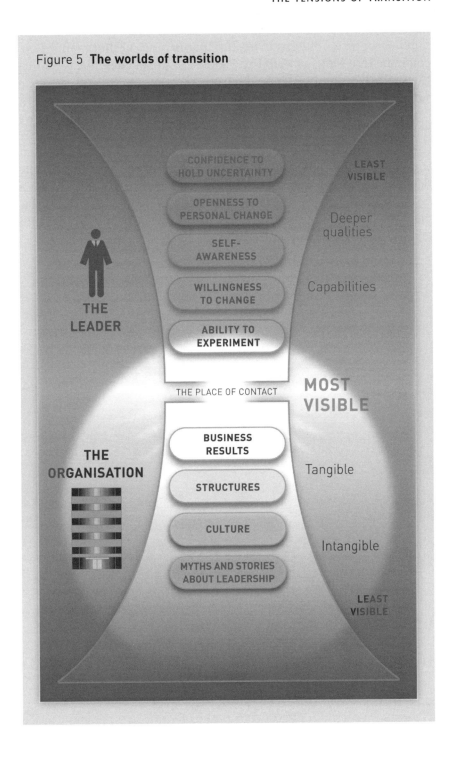

numbers or we don't." Structure, the "hardwiring" of the organisation, comes next in terms of visibility. People can usually describe the structures, processes and systems which are in operation. Indeed, these are sometimes perceived to be the sum total of what an organisation is. Culture is less visible than structure but is no less important, as we have said above. Finally, what leaders stand for in truth is frequently the least visible of the four. Leaders are often so busy acting that they neglect the significance and symbolism of their actions. In the diagram above we represent the different levels of visibility of each "core area." The greater the leader's extension into the less visible areas of culture and stance, the greater his impact on the people around him and the more successful his transition.

4

The inner qualities of leaders

Some leaders succeed in transition better than others. This is an observable fact. Given similar starting points, some leaders manage themselves and their organisation more competently down the rapids of transition. We have observed and supported a large number of leaders in transition, and it is evident to us that some cope better than others with contexts of similar levels of challenge.

What are successful transitions?

What is success? By the time they have been through Surviving, successful leaders appear to be comfortable in their role. They are at ease, and this communicates itself to people around them. The transition has progressed at a steady pace, without frustrating delays. People in the organisation are keen to work with the leader. There is a feeling of anticipation about the future and of momentum in the present. The leader feels accepted by the organisation. The organisation feels confident. There is a feeling of a natural fit between the two. The leader has understood how the business works. He has already a sense of the direction for the future. In sum, by the end of transition, the consensus of opinion is that the appointment was a good one.

But not all leaders manage their transition well. When this is the case, the mood is noticeably different. Instead of a wanting to work together, there is reticence and doubt. Instead of togetherness with the leader, there is a tangible gap. Instead of acceptance, there is critical judgement. Instead of a growing sense of competence, there is a lack of grip in the leader and self-doubt. Most leaders who experience such difficulties struggle through the transition period, and remain in post. They are, however, unlikely to lead as effectively as their peers who managed transitions successfully. The optimism which people started with gradually corrodes and seeps away. What could have been great becomes ordinary. The promise of a new era which the appointment offered evaporates step by step, and people gradually downgrade their expectations of the leader's tenure.

Downgrading of expectations is significant

How frequent is this evolution? In our experience, a fair percentage (approximately one-third, based on qualitative soundings and a small number of internal unpublished company studies) of all new leadership appointments disappoint. The great majority of these fall into the downgraded expectations category described above. In these cases, the organisations usually tolerate what they have for a number of years, before moving the leader on. But a fair number of leaders are moved out quickly or are parked into project-style roles, until they can be exited. While we are not aware of any reliable studies about the precise failure rate of new leaders, our own soundings suggest that as many as 10 percent of all leaders are judged within the first year to not be up to scratch. In often high-profile cases reported in the media, companies terminate leaders' contracts "by mutual agreement" alleging "differences over strategy," "personality clashes" or "cultural incompatibility."

Whatever the stated justification, the more humdrum truth is that the leaders' transitions have collapsed: a common explanation is the person appointed was making too big a jump – what appeared like a bold move (for example, by appointing a leader from a different sector altogether) turns out to have been an overly risky one, involving too big a gap in knowledge and understanding to be filled within a reasonable time.

The inner strengths of the leader are decisive

The most significant reason for these stark failures (and many of the "downgraded expectations" cases mentioned above) is that the leaders did not have the inner strengths sufficiently developed at the time they were in transition. We distinguish between two levels of strengths, the transition capabilities and the deeper qualities.

The transition capabilities

We know that leaders are more successful in making role transitions when they use and display three capabilities. These are:

Self-awareness
This means you have a balanced view of where you are effective and where your shortcomings are. It means you are able to hear feedback about yourself with interest and engage without defensiveness in a conversation about yourself with others. You can accept praise for what you do well and know how and why it is that you do it well. You know which of your shortcomings you need to compensate for and you know which ones can realistically be changed. You work with

enthusiasm on the latter and make sure the former do not disable you or those around you. You believe it is important to understand what makes you tick and are curious about yourself without being self-indulgent. In the Transition Tools Table on p. 157 you will find tools to help you with this under "Tools to open and learn."

A willingness to change

This means you tend to see the world – and especially your work – as an opportunity for you to get to know more about yourself and to expand who you know yourself to be. You don't define changing something about yourself as equal to a deficiency that should be hidden until it is improved. Your interest in change is driven by a desire to maximise your talents and abilities. You hold a perception about yourself which is of someone who can respond to different situations and people in a variety of ways; you value flexibility and adaptability – of thinking and acting. Your tendency is to see personal change as exciting, often tough to do in practice, but usually worth the effort. In the Tools section you will find tools to help you with this under "Tools to diagnose and prioritise."

Ability to experiment

This means you are ready to take risks with how you behave and operate. You know the nature of risk taking is not to know how an action will turn out, and you ride the uncertainties of experimenting with realistic caution coupled with optimism. Your self-esteem is secure enough for you to know that things you try out may mean you end up with egg on your face – and that looking silly is not life threatening. You know how to laugh at yourself and when to take yourself seriously – but usually you have a healthy sense of the surreal and of your own place in an, at times, crazy world. You hold a belief that courage is an essential attribute of leadership and don't confuse it with self-seeking heroics. Your own sense of personal status and authority is more bound up in actions that mostly serve a larger goal than your own ends – which is why experiments and uncertainty don't threaten the chance of your next promotion. In fact, in your experience, they have led to it. In the Tools Table you will find tools to help you with this under "Tools to practise and change behaviour."

If these three descriptions have you closing the book now ... STOP! Read on.

Of course it's hard for any of us to measure up completely to such descriptions of behaviour. But think for a moment of what you are facing as you move into a new role: your self-awareness has been sharpened as a result of the interviews, psychometrics and discussions you have had. You have been the focus of all of these. Although most of the time you were probably in "self-sell" mode, you will have been quizzed about where you see your shortcomings and how you compensate for them. The fact you have chosen to have a new role means you are willing to step out and try something new; you may even have decided to go for a different sector or even way of life than you have been used to so far. You know the world you are about to enter is different from the one you have come from, and that you have to find new ways to meet it. Whilst you feel nervous at times as you think about the new role, mostly you know your usual confidence and experience will see you through. As you consider where you are now, you can begin to balance these three capabilities of self-awareness, the willingness to change and ability to experiment. You may even realise that you are already expanding your capability as you move into your new role.

The deeper qualities

What inner strengths permit a leader to develop his self-awareness, his willingness to change and his ability to experiment? Some leaders develop the capabilities faster and more thoroughly than others. Why might this be?

Through observation and research, we have concluded that two deeper qualities are needed. These are the pre-conditions for the development of the capabilities above. We have found that these deeper qualities can also be developed. They are openness to personal change and confidence to hold uncertainty.

We have come to see that these two qualities in particular are critical during transition. They shape the outcome of the transition, successful or otherwise. Leaders ask us if they will need these qualities after the phase of transition is completed. Our answer is "You bet!" These qualities are essential to leadership (as opposed to management), and characterise the modern leader. Let us now explore each of the qualities.

The openness to personal change
On the face of it, asserting that new leaders in post need to be able to learn may sound mildly uninteresting if somewhat paradoxical to you: Learn? Learn? All of us do it all the time, so what's the big deal? And aren't leaders appointed precisely because they are assumed to "know"? Don't bosses (and their colleagues) want leaders who know what they need to know from the start? Of course, leaders do need to

know lots of things about how business or administration works (in general), about how to manage a business or division (in general), about people and what motivates them (in general), and about the management of change (in general). But should they also know lots about the specifics of this business, this organisation, this sector, before they even open the door?

Unless he is appointed from within, it is simply not possible for the leader to know in advance the specifics of the organisation he is taking charge of and the business it operates in. There is a mass to learn. We described at some length the pressures to learn in the Arriving phase. Time is short and the leader knows he needs to get on top of the "data" as fast as possible. Indeed, he even knows that it is his rate of absorption of the new data which is on the critical path to the organisation getting moving. Transitions always slow things down, until the leader can catch up. A significant minority of leaders are appointed from within an existing senior team, and therefore know the organisation and its business. In this situation, the leader normally needs to take in and make sense of much less data, but this situation brings with it other challenges – how can the leader recreate a relationship of appropriate distance with people who were his peers but are now his subordinates? How can he decide his loyalties to his superiors as well as to his subordinates? How can he reshape his image internally as the new boss? This is not necessarily a cakewalk.

Most of us tend to think of the result of learning as "knowing more" by the end of the process compared to the beginning. We picture our brains as a vessel that we fill with facts. That is the kind of learning we did at school or university. The leader needs to do lots (and lots) of it in the early stages of transition, as we have seen, but being good at it is not sufficient to guarantee success. What the leader needs to learn to succeed in transition is different from learning facts about the world "out there." He also needs to be able to change himself, that is, his beliefs, his attitudes, his behaviours and his feelings. In transition, successful leaders engage willingly to develop themselves, conscious that their change is one of the motors of the change of the organisation they are now responsible for.

Why is this so? Beyond the need to learn new information in transition, the leader needs to find his place in the organisation. He must learn how he is going to comport himself to be effective in the new context. Being as he was before (in his previous role and organisation), and doing as he did before, doesn't work. It just doesn't. Replica leaders do not adapt. New contexts demand different ways. For the leader to be able to sense what new ways will work as he enters the new organisation, he needs to allow the organisation to enter him. He needs to open himself to allow himself to be changed by the organisation, as well as requiring the organisation to open itself, for him to have an impact on it. For the leader to do this, to consciously welcome into himself something as powerful as an organisational culture, he requires openness to personal change.

The confidence to hold uncertainty
The leader is confronted by uncertainty in transition

When managers are leading, they guide their organisation into an uncertain future. They add unique value by mobilising, inspiring and guiding their people to confront challenges that they have (by definition) never confronted before. Leaders take people into zones of uncertainty and risk, where necessarily very little is known about what will work. The second prime quality that we have identified as being essential for "better" transitions is the ability to hold high levels of uncertainty. In transition, the level of uncertainty (prevalent in all organisational life) is heightened by the fact that a leader is new, and neither she nor anyone else can know if she has the qualities to succeed and whether she will fit in.

Consider the following quotes you read in section 2 (Arriving, Surviving, Thriving):

For the first time in my career I was waking up in the middle of the night and worrying about the company and the job. I had never done that before. Notwithstanding all the qualities I think I've got, I was being pushed right to the edge and feeling slightly helpless ... I was feeling at that moment like I didn't know whether it's going to turn out good or not.

... How could I say to my boss what I was going through? I needed him to go on believing in me and trusting that I knew what I was doing.

... And, you start to really question yourself as to whether you are even capable of doing this job.

... Learning about the downsides of an image, whether it's a true or untrue reflection of what the real me is, I thought was very valuable. I could see, "Oh yes, some people could quite easily see me as cold,

Figure 6 **The worlds of transition**

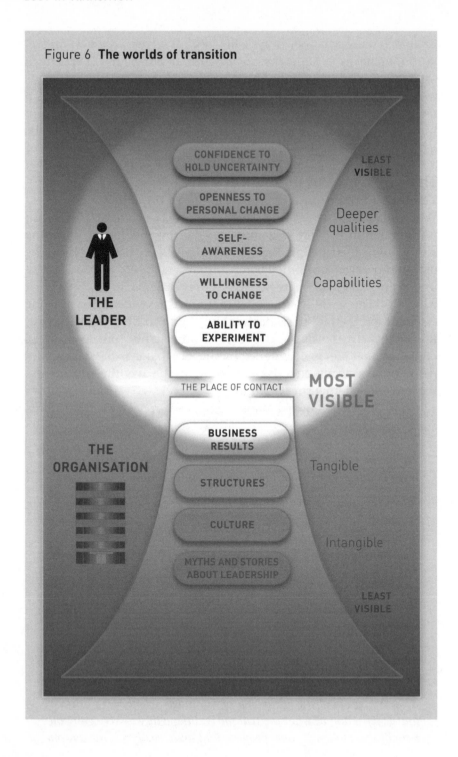

disinterested in the people and softer issues of the workforce, uncompromising." Whether I am or whether I'm not those things, I could be seen by others as that.

... You can't be somebody who loves to be loved by everybody. I was trying to be too much one of the boys. But then I'd yo-yo back into I'm going to be very tough and hard and it was a bit confusing for people.

The quotes reveal that the leaders felt uncertain about a range of questions:

• Who they really are.
• Whom they are expected to be by the organisation they have joined.
• Whether these two are in acceptable harmony: will the person they believe they are be up to the person they are expected to be?
• What if this person is just not good enough for the organisation?
• Will they be able to tough their way through? This has worked for them in the past. Why shouldn't it work now? What is different about this job change?
• If they know whom they are expected to be, and there is a gap with who they are, can they change this person fast enough to meet the expectations before they are seen to be a failure?

The three capabilities for transition are most visible and obviously open to influence. Beyond fear of challenge, we confidently assert that you can become better in these three areas of capability. In section 5 below, we provide you with a number of tools designed to do precisely that. You will strengthen the two deeper qualities of leadership in transition, which are less visible and easily measurable, by undertaking this development work over time. With the diagram below, we are drawing attention to the different level of visibility of the capabilities and qualities. The greater the leader's endeavour to strengthen the deeper qualities, which are less visible and malleable, the greater the impact of her leadership and the quality of her transition.

Awareness of self and of the context

How much "self-awareness" (the person I think I am) and "context-awareness" (the person I am expected to be by the organisation) do most new leaders in post have? In our experience, and generalising for the purposes of making the point, most leaders in transition have:

145

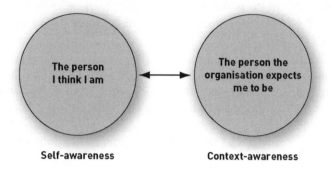

Self-awareness   Context-awareness

Relatively low self-awareness. They may have undergone one or other psychometric test and may have been told they are an "ESTJ" or a "Chairman" type or whatever. As a result, they may have developed some idea as to what "type" of person they are; this knowledge can be useful, as far as it goes. The main problem with these "types" is that they can feel wooden and stereotypical to many managers. Once a manager knows his type, what then? Is that all he needs to (and can) know about himself?

In our experience, most managers who reach positions of seniority in the forties have done relatively little exploration of themselves. Why? They have usually not needed to. Their job has been to act competently within frameworks established by their bosses. They have usually been given very clear guidance about the "what" (the results they needed to deliver or achieve), and also about the "how," at least in terms of the values that would need to be respected. All this direction came from above. In the more senior role they have now reached, the manager now needs to shape, if not decide, a large part of both the "what" and the "how." Where should the manager look for guidance to decide these? The manager will be guided in large measure by his own preferences, values and inclinations. To know these, the manager needs to look into himself, which is why self-awareness becomes more and more important as the manager rises higher and higher up the ladder.

High motivation to learn more about themselves if this can be done in a safe way. In our experience, once senior managers understand that knowing more about themselves is critical to their success in their new position, they invariably get interested! But this is not necessarily where they look first of all – they are usually more tempted by the cerebral offerings from classical business schools in such

146

domains as strategy, planning and operations management. The task as they see it is to sharpen up their mental tools to help them to solve problems "out there," to cope with the fact that the problems they now need to deal with are more complex and more intractable. What *all* the leaders require, even if they are not aware of it, is a deeper and more expanded self-awareness. Some continue doing things as they have done them before, finding it hard to let go of their existing identity. But other leaders turn speedily and courageously to do the tough work of growing self-awareness, once they become aware that they need to. This work needs to be done in safe conditions however, for two important reasons. The first reason is that, as we made clear in our opening section about myths, there are many prejudices in our society and in our organisations which militate against leaders making themselves vulnerable by acknowledging publicly that there are things they do not know, about themselves and about the context they are in; the prevailing myth is the all-knowing, all-seeing, all-capable leader. So smart managers are discreet about the self-awareness work they are doing. The second reason is that the work itself is delicate. Opening out, exploring, challenging give rise in the manager to many fears: that he may not be up to the job, that he will be "found out," that the person he thought he was is not the one that shows up to work each day. Smart managers are caring about themselves as well as others. They tackle their development work with vigour but also mindful that work on oneself requires tenderness and care.

Few skills to build awareness. They have neither had a priority need for such skills in their career to date, nor have they been taught them. So, why should we expect them to have them? We have found that most senior people have few skills in the area, and that, understandably, they struggle to grow their self-awareness without support (assuming of course that they want to). But, with the right support, we have also found that managers can develop many of the skills they need within a number of months. Let us take the skill to negotiate with one's boss, a key skill in transition. As we have seen in section 3, many new leaders have a poorly defined mission, and are not clear about what is expected of them (in terms of change), nor able to know whether any targets they have been given are achievable. They sometimes come to realise that to "just get on with it!" will not work. Within a relatively short space of time, and with the right support, they can become more competent to engage with their boss or the head of HR to get a clearer idea of what the expectations are of them, as manager and as people. They acquire the skills to dare to go back, ask questions and assert their beliefs, in the service of clarifying their mission.

Becoming more aware of "the person I think I am" and "the person the organisation expects me to be" is one of the main jobs to be done by every leader in transition. And of course, nothing stays permanent for long. Both of the above will necessarily evolve through time, which is to be expected and reckoned with.

The dance of transition enables coming together
As the leader learns more about the organisation she has charge of, and about its challenges and problems, the leader is changed. As she brings the reality of the organisation into herself, she becomes part of the organisation. But by moving towards the organisation (which she needs to do if she is going to successfully transition), she is adapting to her environment. This is the dance of transition, holding one's identity and being adaptable, at the same time. By entering into this dance, the leader will change some of her views of the world, and even some of her beliefs. If this goes too far, as we have seen with the Loyalty tension, the leader's boss may feel that she has "gone native." Of course, the leader must balance appropriately and retain her identity as she adapts, or she will be of less use to the organisation.

To succeed in transition, leaders need to be able to "hold" the uncertainty they feel about their own adequacy for the role they have accepted. "Holding" means being able to carry on without being able to get rid of the uncertainty, day in, day out. "Holding" means keeping faith that you are right for the role, even if things are tough, and you are making mistakes (which you have to do, within reason, to learn). "Holding" means continuing to act with composure, when there are no established rules or guidelines, but only uncharted territory. "Holding" means staying out in front as the leader, accepting that this is precisely the place the organisation needs you to be in.

We know from experience that managers new to leadership roles are surprised (and challenged) by the need for them to hold uncertainty. They are usually unprepared for the depth of uncertainty they will need to hold, about themselves, about their suitability for their role and about the context they are entering. They are often not schooled to expect that uncertainty comes with the territory called leadership. *"If uncertainty is so all-pervasive in leadership, why am I expected to appear so certain as a leader?"*, they might well ask. This contradiction is one of the constants of leadership roles. Followers prefer their leaders to relieve them of uncertainty, and to answer unknowable questions about the future. Leaders cannot do this, in fact, and should not attempt to. What leaders can and should do is to accept the inevitability of uncertainty, hold it and encourage their people to live with it. Leaders can learn to hold uncertainty better, and we shall be describing some tools and hints about this in the next section.

And there is uncertainty in the organisation too

Just as the leader is entering into a major period of uncertainty during transition, so too is the organisation. The arrival of a new leader is probably the most threatening, unsure and unsafe period in any worker's time in an organisation. And it can also be a period full of uncertain promise. The kinds of questions people ask themselves are:

- Will I have a place in the organisation the new leader wants to create?

- Will I still have a job that I value?

- Will I lose power? Will I lose status?

- Will the new leader fulfil all my expectations?

- Will I have the skills that are required in the future? Will I find that I am no longer competent?

- Will we finally be able to turn the corner and realise our objectives?

- Will the new leader bring in his "own people" who will carve out powerful roles for themselves, at my expense?

During transition, people in an organisation with a new leader do not know how much overlap there will be between the two circles below. This creates uncertainty, and usually anxiety.

People in organisations are often unskilled at handling the uncertainty that accompanies the arrival of a new leader. Many have learnt through experience a number of tricks through which they can gain best advantage in the situation. Lucy Kellaway, a journalist with the *Financial Times*, spelt out five proven strategies which people use to

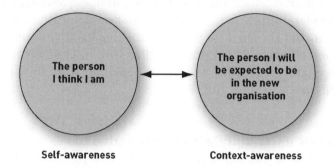

Self-awareness   Context-awareness

help themselves through the transition period with her trademark no-holes-barred style. These were, "Monster brown-nosing," "Playing the wise old owl," "Planning your exit route," "Becoming a full-time gossip" and "Keep your head down and get on with your job" (her preferred strategy).* Of course, by employing these strategies, people reinforce and perpetuate the usual way of carrying on during organisational transitions: survive as best you can, and mind your back. This is the very same strategy that leaders often employ to get through the turbulent first months of their tenure, as we described in section 2.

Which people can choose to resolve in different ways

People in organisations undergoing transition undoubtedly have choices about how to act: they can choose to facilitate the new leader's entry, to impede it or take a neutral approach. They can choose to promote their own position or to support their group or level. How the leader acts will have a bearing on the choices people make, and vice versa. The new leader cannot instruct people how to react. Probably the best he can do, by the way he acts, is to communicate the respect he feels for the situation they are in. We have learnt from William Bridges' work on transitions that all significant change takes its time to work through, and that people in transition cross a mourning period for the old state (what he calls the "neutral zone") before they accept a new state. New leaders in post arrive when people are often still in that mourning period; leaders need to appreciate that people cannot "switch" to the new regime like a light-switch is turned on or off. People are holding onto loyalties for the old state, and often the previous leader, which need to wane slowly before new loyalties can be

* "Play your cards right while a new leader reshuffles his pack," *Financial Times,*
  Monday 21 November 2005.

entered into. They alone can accomplish this transition, in their own way and own time. If they look into themselves at this same time, leaders may find they too are feeling loyalty to their previous job and company. They can feel that they have not quite left the previous state, and therefore have not quite "arrived" in the new one.

Seven ways for the leader to facilitate the transition in the organisation

While respecting this in-between state of affairs, leaders can create a context that makes it easier for people to accomplish their own transition. Here is a range of areas where leaders can choose to act to create such a context, mindful that the balance they strike must be appropriate to the context they are in.

1   They can from the start communicate who they are and what their remit is, balancing change with stability. In so doing, they will be cautious not to criticise past leaders and their policies.

2   They can create bonds with their people while maintaining appropriate distance. Being themselves from the start, while respecting the demands of their position, helps leaders to engage.

3   They can request their subordinates to help them learn, while also seeking to give something valuable in return. By openly recognising the limits of their knowledge, leaders are usually seen as being strong. By "winging it," leaders usually lose credibility.

4   They can establish ground rules about how they want people to be involved in taking decisions, balancing imposition with facilitation. Leaders communicate this information unconsciously in any event – is it not preferable to have a worked-out and explicit position? Yes.

5   They can slow down or speed up the change of their organisation, in line with their growing competence as the leader. Everybody knows that nothing is to be gained by hanging about, but equally going off "half-cock" can be a killer.

6 They can remove or keep people, balancing the need for change with the opportunities to develop people. How a new leader deals with people at the start is never forgotten, and sometimes never forgiven.

7 They can ensure that they actively attend to the image of loyalty they are giving to both their bosses and their subordinates. Leaders are inevitably in an "in-between" position. Letting go of one end of the rope is a quick recipe for a short tenure as a leader.

In the next section about tools, we will describe further ways to manage the 8 Tensions we described in section 3.

Can the inner qualities be developed in transition?

Yes. The transition capabilities and the deeper qualities can be developed through intentional development work, involving experimentation.

The place to start is the three transition capabilities of self-awareness, willingness to change and ability to experiment. In section 5, you will find a selection of tools that will enable you to strengthen these. Each of the transition capabilities is deeper and more complex than a managerial skill. Each is partially determined by our natural self which tends to be biologically fixed. But each is also shaped by our profoundly anchored habits, which have grown out of the confrontation between our natural self and experience. By the time we reach adulthood, these habits are deeply ingrained; to change them requires dedication, patience with oneself and realism. That is the real work of leadership development.

The leader will strengthen his deeper qualities of openness to personal change and confidence to hold uncertainty by undertaking the development work above. The more self-aware a leader is, the more he can exploit his natural openness to personal change, and the more able he is to know what things cause him to be anxious and what antidotes he can apply. The more willing a leader is to change, the more he is open to a range of aspects of experience, inner and outer, and the more secure his self-concept. This grows his confidence to hold uncertainty. Finally, the greater his ability to experiment, the more confidently the leader will reach out to develop less known areas

Figure 7 **The worlds of transition**

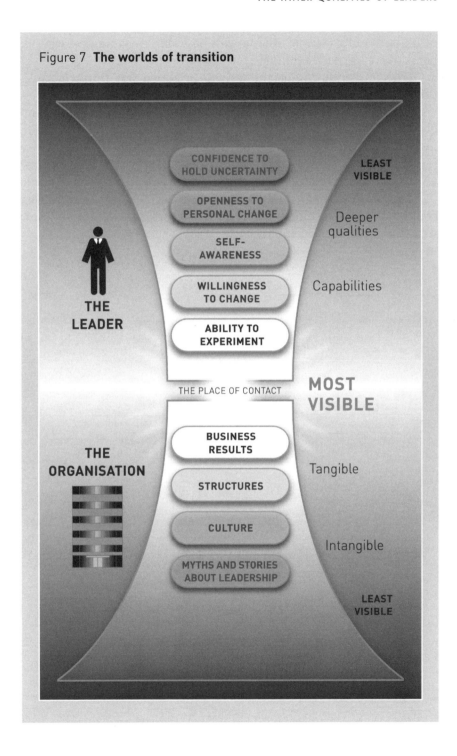

of himself and the more able he will be to build viable new ways of being in an era of uncertainty.

To become truly competent at managing their way through transitions, leaders need to recognise and value both the visible and the less visible factors which are at play within themselves (the capabilities and deeper qualities) and within their organisations (from business results to the leader's stance). In the diagram above, we illustrate the importance for the leader to consciously manage in parallel his own development and that of the "core areas" of his transition in his organisation.

May we encourage you now to explore a wide range of tools that could make a lot of difference to how you are in transition and how well you arrive, survive and thrive.

5

The tools
for transition

In this section we describe a range of tools to help you meet the personal and organisational issues your transition is likely to throw at you. These are tried and tested methods which will equip you to think, act and reflect well in this transition. They can be used to understand what is happening for you personally (usually internally and silently), to make sense of what is going on around you with your boss, team and colleagues:

- What can you do that avoids repeating past, unhelpful actions – which may have been very effective then – but might not "fit" in this context?
- How do you cope with the avalanche of new information, people and issues?
- Where do you begin when your knowledge about who is who and how to get things done is the size of a pea?
- How quickly is anyone expecting you to get your feet under the table?
- How long will you be allowed to be new for?

These are the questions that the Tools for Transition are designed to help you answer – and we hope also the hundreds of other questions which will be racing around in your mind as you think about your new role.

Don't just read it ... DO IT!

Reading about ideas, approaches and techniques is a start – but it doesn't change much. If you really want to lead yourself and others through this transition we encourage you to act on what you find here. You will change little unless you convert your intentions and aspirations to actions that impact the world around you. Support to act differently is vital – even for the most macho of risk takers. So start here and now.

How to use the tools

Transitions affect who you are *and* what you do *and* how you act. In other words they impact you *psychologically* as well as behaviourally through questions about your self-esteem and self-image; and they challenge your judgement and capacity to act soundly in a new context. We have called these dimensions respectively Tools directed to Self and Tools directed to Context. Across the top of the table you will find the three transition capabilities, each of which is supported by one or more tools according to whether you want to address Self or Context.

Figure 8 **Transition tools table: Choices for change**

TOOLS DIRECTED TO:	SELF-AWARENESS Tools to open and learn	WILLINGNESS TO CHANGE Tools to diagnose and prioritise	ABILITY TO EXPERIMENT Tools to practice and change behaviour
SELF	**Journaling & Freefall**	**Tensions: Diagnosis** **Leadership Transition Questionnaire**	**Tensions: Experimenting** **Feedback** **Support**
CONTEXT	**Context scanning**	**Core areas**	**Story circles**

◄──── ENQUIRY & EXPERIMENTS ────►
Key practices throughout transition

Personal Style Questionnaire

Wherever you start, and if you do nothing else with the tools, we recommend strongly that you complete the Personal Style Questionnaire (PSQ) in the Appendix. This will give you clear sight of yourself and how you will be likely to operate in this transition. You will identify which behaviours you will be drawn to in the 8 Tensions and so how you and others are likely to experience your leadership at this time. You will also find out more about which tensions you will be blind to or less interested in using and what impact this might have given the context in which you are leading. We know that leaders who can appropriately match their leadership to the context are more effective faster in getting their feet under the table. Once you have this information about yourself you will be better equipped to describe why you operate as you do, see where to change if at all, and avoid the time wasting effort of trying to understand whether it's you or them that are the problem – an inevitable question for all transitions!

Choosing the right tool

Once you have completed the PSQ, you will know more about where to direct your learning efforts: inwardly to yourself, outwards to the context – or both? You will see that Enquiry and Experiments are key practices whichever tool you decide to use. Both these approaches underpin self-awareness, change and living well with uncertainty. They are both practical approaches – tools – as well as more deeply embedded attitudes to how you lead. We strongly encourage you to weave them through the months of your transition – and hopefully beyond.

Because we know the first weeks and months of transition are a whirlwind time, we have used below some of the commonest questions asked by transitioning leaders as pointers for using the tools. If you already know which tools are likely to be useful, skip what follows and get going!

Which way is up? If you are submerged with information about the organisation, its issues and the problems you are tasked with sorting, you will probably welcome some perspectives on the context. Go to Context Scanning where you will find a diagnostic tool to sort and sift the confusion of experience and data.

The Core Areas tool is another one which will tell you more about where your attention and activity is going and whether these are the right places given your context.

Is it me or is it them? Yes, paranoia is as alive and well in transitions as it is at other times of change! If your confidence feels low and you are doubting whether you will ever feel competent again, go to the Freefall tool. Here you have a tool that can silence the inner critic and liberate you from the tiring and endless swirl of confusing thoughts which still seem to be in your head in the small hours of the morning. Dumping down what you are thinking clears your head and makes space for fresh thoughts.

How long can I be new for? All new leaders feel the pressure to deliver and perform. Being new buys you some time – but not forever. Deciding where and how to intervene is watched and noted by others with interest, frustration and sometimes anxiety. Disturbing conventions and bringing in new ways of doing things are easier when you first arrive: tolerance and forgiveness become less and less available the further into your transition you go. Some tools involve you *and* others so this is a chance to exploit your newness with them. The Story Circles tool brings you into conversation with your team by directly confronting the question of transition – for you and them – and what experience you all have of how to manage this. By opening up the topic you can find out what people around you need from you, from each other and how they are finding what you are doing so far. Combine this tool later in your transition with Feedback and you will have the data you need to change your own behaviour and how you work with your team.

Will I ever fit in here? Despite your excitement at getting this role, it is common to find that how you like to work – your style – seems at odds with how the organisation expects you to work. Welcome to culture clash – or culture gulf. Either way, you are wondering how you can find a way through which will not compromise your ways of working which you know are successful with the need to fit enough to be accepted. Turn to the PSQ and use it to look at your less preferred ends of each tension. Use the tensions tool then to diagnose the range of opportunities (and possible risks) if you were to manage the tension differently. Also use the Tensions tool to identify the behaviours you will need to experiment with if you are to strengthen your less-developed pole. Combine it with Feedback to find out more about how people in this organisation really see and value – or not – your ways of operating. The Enquiry tool will give you a structure to understand these experiences better and Experiments give you a plan for how to tackle them.

I don't need tools; I need time! OK, skip this section for now. Use what you have read so far to guide you and return to the tools later when you meet a situation that you feel less well equipped to handle – they will still be here waiting.

Sustaining yourself: Finding the right support to survive and thrive

In the opening section of the book we described the myths of transition. Many of them centred on the commonest myth that leaders need to be heroes – strong, go-it-alone, self-sufficient, tireless individuals who can take whatever their new role throws at them and still operate at the peak of their ability. Our research emphatically says this is not the reality and that leaders can employ a wide range of support mechanisms to sustain them through transition – and even later through the continuing demands of complex leadership roles. This tool describes a range of ways to sustain yourself so that your energy, focus and purpose remain alive and healthy – and you personally thrive at work.

Other people

✓ It's hard to manage what you cannot – or do not – discuss. Find a trusted person who will be interested in you and what you are doing and who has the skills to enquire with you into your experience, and use them as a sounding board through the early months of your transition. Focus on your internal *and* external experience.

✓ If you are in a new sector or industry and want to get to know it fast, meet the people who can give you the lowdown honestly on how it really works. Usually these will be older people who have been around in it a while, or the people who are closest to the coalface. Customers too can offer you straight-from-the-horses-mouth data on what they experience. Bring a group together and get them talking.

✓ Most leaders are curious about how they are doing and how they are going down in the organisation. This kind of information is a support because it fills the vacuum of paranoia. Ask your boss and your team. Use the Eavesdropping Feedback tool with your team and construct some simple questions to help your boss tell you what *you* want to know about, as well as what he wants to tell you. Make sure some of your questions directly ask for what you are doing well.

Time

✓ However capable you are, you still only have 24 hours in the day. First, remind yourself that you are not paid to work all of them, then, as soon as you arrive in your new role, allocate yourself a minimum of two hours a week in your diary. Label this time Transition Strategy.

Use it to:

- Make sense of what is happening to you (Freefall and Journaling) and/or
- Make sense of what you need to do (Context Scanning and Core Areas tools).
- Put an electric fence around this time for at least three months and watch how more effective you become.
- Ask other people to remind you when you are becoming a headless chicken.

Physical

Exercise boosts energy and makes you feel more alive. Moving your body also moves your mind: if you find the same thoughts and feelings coming back like a bad dream, shift your body physically. Even if you are not a fitness fan, there are still some simple things you can do every day to move your body more and refuel your brain and stamina:

✓ Get off the tube one stop earlier than your destination.
✓ Get out of the office and in the fresh air through the day. Hold meetings at a local café and walk there.
✓ Take ten deep breaths in and out when you feel up against it: Buddhists believe ten breaths can change your state of mind.

Knowledge

Knowledge gives us control; feeling out of control by not knowing (what needs to be done, what needs to be known, who to influence, etc) is one of the commonest experiences of the early weeks of transition.

✓ Make two columns.
✓ Write down all your questions in the left-hand one, however trivial or however complex.
✓ Choose the five that you believe would give you greatest comfort to get some answers to.
✓ In the right-hand column write down where and who are most likely to know – at least initially.
✓ Go and begin to find out. Being systematic and purposeful in themselves helps you feel in control, even if some of your questions may be unanswerable immediately.

And finally …

✓ Make a commitment that you will do ONE thing from the suggestions above.

Do-Be-Do-Be-Do … Which comes first? Thinking or doing?

Introduction

We've made regular mention in this book of the importance of balancing both ends of the 8 Tensions. And in section 4 on the inner qualities of leaders, we describe how the leader and his organisation need to learn to

161

do a "dance" together, in which both allow themselves to be influenced and changed by the other. By now you will have got the message that transitions are a time for combining reflection, decisions and action, ideally in the right proportion; the "either this … or that …" approach is less useful in complex and fast moving times. Too much reflection and you may risk being seen as indecisive; if you act too quickly you may take the organisation down the wrong road. Reflection *and* decisiveness are both needed. So how do you arrive at the "right" decision?

Using your best judgement

Nordstrom, the US department store which consistently reports the highest levels of customer service of all retailers, has condensed its employee handbook into one sentence: *use your best judgement at all times*. What Nordstrom is asking for from its employees is the right action that comes about when careful reflection is balanced with considered decision making, or as they call it, your best judgement.

For leaders who are used to being decisive and who may even have made their reputations on their decisive style, the deliberate practice of reflection as a skill in its own right, comes as something of a surprise. Enquiring into, reflecting on and discovering more about the situation you are in are fundamental to the development of good judgement. Many of the leaders we know are bright, fast thinkers who can mentally process large amounts of information with impressive speed. In fact they thrive on it. So how does reflection and enquiry fit with this capability? What can slower – or possibly different – mental processing offer the new in-post leader that his usual way of operating might not?

One of the questions that new leaders always face is: how do I know what to listen to and what to ignore? How do I decide what is important here? These questions highlight the difficulty of using your judgement when the context is not fully understood or known to you and the importance of knowing where you can find the most useful information.

Central to our work in developing leaders is to grow their capacity to enquire skilfully into what is going on around them. This is more than just asking questions – although that's a great start! It involves asking particular types of questions in a sequence that is likely to bring you to a position of better judgement about how to act. At the same time it helps to sort out the great muddle between fact, fiction, reality and theory. We call this the **Cycle of Enquiry**. This is how it works.

Figure 9 **The Cycle of Enquiry**

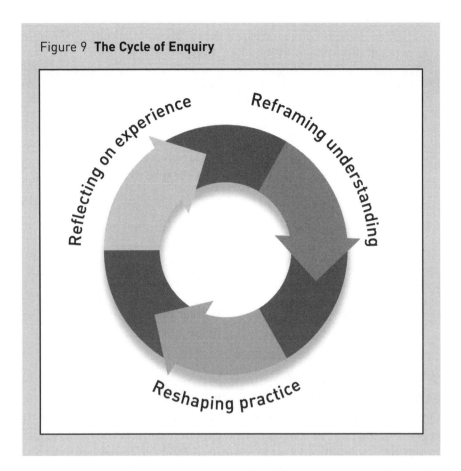

1. Enquiring into experience: Drawing out and getting below the surface story

The world each of us experiences is unique – even though we often act and talk as though we all see things the same way. How we make sense of the work we do, deciding what to do, working out how to operate are all choices we make that are peculiar to each of us. So when you come to reflect on what is happening to you – your experiences – and as you try to make sense of them, the chances are high that your views will not be like others. In fact, as the new leader arriving into a new role, and maybe new organisation, it is very likely that your experiences will be quite different from anyone else's. So a start point is to ask questions – enquire – more deeply into what is going on in those experiences, so that you can create a thorough understanding of where you yourself might be muddling fact, fiction and reality.

The kinds of questions to ask yourself – or even better to get someone else to ask you – look like these:

Tell me what's on your mind?	This is what I've heard you say?
Can you tell me more about that?	Can you give me a metaphor for this?
What are you not telling me?	Does this prompt any image?
What were you feeling then?	It sounds like you are now feeling …
What other perspectives else to add?	Is there anything might there be?

2. Reframing understanding: Testing out the obvious explanations, seeking alternative explanations

Once you have drawn out the key areas of the experience you want to reflect on, the next step is to put that experience under the microscope: to test the explanations you give yourself (and others) about it, to see what other likely explanations there could be for it by challenging your own assumptions and beliefs about that experience. One of the ways you can learn to become more adaptable and responsive to your context, is to use the Cycle of Enquiry to challenge your habitual ways of thinking. This is the part of the Cycle which can be uncomfortable. You may find yourself resisting alternative explanations or fighting to justify the sense you are making of your experience. When you do allow your thinking to expand you open yourself to new and different interpretations that lead to fresh perspectives and actions. In the Context tool we describe the limiting ways in which we like to process information and how misleading this can be in new situations. This step is the one that helps you break out of those self-limiting ways of thinking. These are the kinds of questions to help you reframe your understanding:

Why do you think happened?	How else could you describe this?
What evidence do you have?	How would [xxx] explain what happened here?
Is that the only interpretation?	What pairings could be at play here?
What other reasons might there be?	What stage of transition is this?
Does this remind you of other situations?	How else could you check this out?

3. Reshaping practice: Continuing your enquiry through experiments

Having worked through the two previous stages of the reflection and enquiry into your experience you are now ready to apply the insights to how you go about your work as a new leader – what we call reshaping your practice. This is the step where you firm up on how you might change some of what you are doing.

When some strongly held assumptions are challenged – in the way you might have done in stage 2 above – and replaced by others that are more up to date and relevant to this context, you realise that that the actions arising from these assumptions will also need to change. Hence the need now to reflect on how else you might act.

Here are some of the questions that will help you reshape your practice:

What do you want to do now?	What will you commit to doing?
What might you be avoiding? How can you support yourself to act differently?	Is this a realistic expectation? How will you track your new practice?
What are the risks/rewards	Where will you look for feedback?
How important is this to you?	How will you hold yourself to account?

Watchpoints for success

✓ Don't expect to master this approach immediately – it repays with regular and continuous practice.

✓ Use it anywhere and in any setting: the whole of your life is open to enquiry!

✓ Remember that enquiry is not a substitute for action, nor is only action the basis of sound leadership.

Scanning the context

Think of a time you travelled to a country for the first time. If you can, remember also the first time you were in a country where not only the language was different form your own, but so was the alphabet. All is fine while you are still in the international airport – signs still in several languages, local staff speaking your language fluently – communication and finding your way about no problem.

But you have to move beyond the airport and find your way about the country. How do you know the taxi driver is charging you the right amount? Is he even taking you in the right direction – or on a round-about route to your hotel? As you travel along the major highway through this unfamiliar country, you look at the passing scene. You notice how rutted and bumpy is the road you are driving on – supposedly a motorway – but with people wandering along the road at the side. You look beyond the road and see highrise blocks with almost every floor flying the national flag and you wonder if it is a national holiday. The taxi driver tries to engage you in conversation but his accent is heavy and you struggle to understand what he is saying. After several embarrassing attempts to talk to him, including sign language, you give up. As you enter the outskirts of the city where you are staying, you join a long queue of traffic apparently paying to be allowed through a checkpoint. You notice children are gathered at the roadside selling local souvenirs. By this time you are probably reaching for your Lonely Planet guide.

If this is a description of your experience of travelling abroad, how did you handle these experiences? How did you explain to yourself the sights you saw? What went through your mind as you compared this country with your own? What kind of tour guide were you for your-self? What was your guidebook unable to explain – or didn't cover?

This experience – of travelling to a foreign land for the first time – has many similarities with arriving in a new role, in a new organisation. The landscape has some points of familiarity – airports seem much the same wherever you go – but the further into the "country" you travel, the greater are the differences you begin to notice. Those early hours and days after you arrive can be exciting, disorientating, stimulating and confusing – not unlike the early period of arriving in a new role! But you will know also that the longer you spend in this foreign land, the more familiar and taken for granted are your experiences. What seemed strange and different at first will, after a time, become normal and everyday. The difference between arriving in a foreign land and arriving in a new role, is that understanding the latter reasonably accurately impacts not only you but many others through the decisions and actions you will need to take. So how can you be your own tour guide and get under the skin of this strange new land?

Understanding the world around us

To answer this we need to take a step back first to appreciate how we make sense of – how we try to understand – the world around us. One of the commonest ways we make sense of difference is to compare it positively or negatively to our existing experience and knowledge. We like to evaluate it – good/bad, useful/worthless, important/insignificant, like me/not like me, sensible/crazy and so on – and filter out those parts that don't match our view of the world. We will draw conclusions about the bumpy, rutted roads: obviously they don't spend much here on the infrastructure. We may equate the taxi driver's inability to speak our language with his absence of education. We see highrise buildings covered in national flags as a sign that the country is nationalistic, patriotic and might conclude that it is more inward than outward looking. We may feel dismayed at the danger to children in being allowed to run freely near so much traffic and decide about the quality of parenting in this land. And so on. Each new sight and experience is evaluated against a personal set of standards and an existing personal "library" of experiences. If the strangeness and newness of experiences feels threatening or we feel less secure with them than usual, the chances are that the comparisons we make will not be favourable ones.

Common ways of sorting what we experience

Karl Weick, a writer on organisations, identifies that we also employ some or all of the following methods to handle the large amounts of new data we face on Arrival:

1 Omit or neglect parts of it.
2 Allow yourself greater tolerance of error in reading and understanding it – or let yourself off the hook if you don't "get it" all.
3 Queue/prioritise the information with greater sternness.
4 Abstract/categorise it.
5 Escape or avoid.

As the load of information increases, we take stronger and stronger steps to manage it. The list above describes the common hierarchy of actions that we tend to adopt as we are faced with growing mountains of data to absorb. Check it out for yourself. Do you use any of these methods to cope with emails, process lengthy reports, sort through your inbox?

Handling load *and* complexity

But we are not only handling information load, we are, at the same time, having to deal with information complexity – the *type* of information we are processing is not simple. When information load *and* complexity come together, we find other means to cope. In these situations we search for the simple, familiar elements of what we are reading or experiencing; in other words, we like to rely on what we know. So we ignore information which challenges what we don't know or which asks us to think in unaccustomed ways. Essentially, Weick says, we are creatures of habit. But the problems these ways of thinking can cause us are potentially dangerous and misleading because they were originally developed in response to other situations than the ones we are facing now. This way of making sense is played out when new leaders arrive and use the "template" of their last organisation as the one against which to making sense of the current one.

But if the goal of Arriving is to get to know the context as thoroughly as possible, so that the right solutions can be identified as a basis for action, then seeing the situation as fully as possible must be the goal. Notice how Weick's list above of what we typically do will have the *opposite* effect, tending to contain and limit our perspectives rather than holding them open and flexible to interpretation.

Remember back to the personal experiences of Arriving in section 2. We described the hidden struggle to deal with feelings of incompetence, lack of confidence and the apparent importance of never showing you are surprised or don't know. We saw how some strategies for coping involve people bluffing their way, acting as though this organisation were the same as every other and resorting to action quickly because "doing something" was reassuring. So the inner world of our experience can also reinforce the tendency to narrow down the world to one that feels more controllable and knowable. Now let's return to the question we posed above: how can you be your own tour guide and get under the skin of this strange new land of the organisation you have joined?

Here's how to do it

To do this exercise you will need to have completed the Personal Style Questionnaire (PSQ) in the Appendix.

1. Begin with yourself. Ask yourself the following questions and answer them with ruthless honesty. If it is easier to do, get a trusted colleague/friend to ask them of you. Draw two columns and fill them in according to the following questions:

- What am I liking (approving of) and not liking (disapproving of) about this organisation so far? List as many things/ people/events/situations as you like, however significant or however small. Alongside each item make a note of why. In your note, include the personal reasons and the business reasons. Both are likely to be present in each.

- Go to the PSQ and identify your preferences in terms of each tension. Then return to your list and see if you can allocate the items on your list to relevant parts of your PSQ profile. Work through all your questions. You may not necessarily have every dimension on your PSQ allocated with comments. Notice though if there is any clustering of comments. This may signal where you are most attentive or where you are most blind!

169

For instance, if under Pace of Change you have a marked preference for "Go fast to perform" you may take from your list comments such as "Take far too long to start doing anything" as an item you don't like. You may also have "Want to ensure they are going to do the right things" as something you do like. Equally you may have put down on one side of your list "Feeling impatient and worried I won't deliver on time."

2. Now use the following list of questions to interrogate your analysis so far. This is designed to highlight where your attention may be going at the moment. Remember: depending on your remit this may be exactly the right focus. Or it may be where you feel most comfortable operating. Developing context sensitivity is about the ability to scan and understand widely regardless of personal comfort. You can continue to do this part alone or consider using your analysis as a basis to check out with a colleague or your team. Context sensitivity gets developed more quickly by hearing the perspectives of others who may already be more familiar with it than you.

- Are your comments clustered mainly into any of the Tensions? If yes, what is the pattern your comments have produced? (For example: Are they mainly about you and your experience? About your boss and how he is operating with you or others? Concerns or evaluations about your team? Are they about your own confusion/clarity? Do they comment on how the organisation operates – its processes, approaches etc?).

- If you have few or no comments in some of the Tensions, how do you explain this? For instance, does it suggest you and the organisation are "in synch" with each other in this aspect? Have you simply not had enough time to experience this Tension yet?

- Where do you think your own PSQ profile – or specific Tensions – are at odds with what you know of the organisation so far? For example, in the Decision Making Tension you have a preference for "Impose" yet your experience so far tells you the organisation is more consultative or even consensual. What are the implications of having a personal and organisational Tension at odds with each other?

- How does this "gap" show up in how you are operating? What else would you need to know and understand to appreciate the organisation's tendency to do things in this way? What beliefs do you hold which get challenged by the difference? How might you adapt your own approaches? Where might you hold to your own preference and "ask" that the organisation adapts to you?

3. **Expanding your awareness of context.** The nature of becoming context sensitive is an ongoing exploration into your organisation: there isn't an end point. The following are all further aids to the important early job:

- Curiosity towards what is going on around you and a good level of self-awareness of your own blind spots (your prejudices and preferences) all help in holding the balance between being open to finding out and the need to take action.

- Re-doing this exercise after four weeks, eight weeks later and again twelve weeks later will provide you with a rich and varied map of your context.

- Share your analysis with others – your team, your boss – and involve them in helping make sense of the context with you.

- You could combine this tool with the Story Circle tool as a way to get others to decode the context for you.

(We would like to acknowledge Edwin Nevis who first introduced us to this metaphor.)

Core areas tool

As we made a point of emphasising in the previous sections, leaders' experience of the first days and weeks of a transition is often dominated by the sheer volume of new things – masses of facts to learn, of relationships to forge and of actions to take (or not). The pressure created by this volume can feel enormously over-powering.

How do you know where to start? How to sift out the important from the less important? How to avoid wasting time on issues of detail? How to discriminate intelligently? In section 3, we described the "core areas" in which leaders will most likely find the priority issues they need to focus on in transition. These were:

1 Agreeing business objectives.
2 Organisation restructuring.
3 Asserting culture.
4 Finding your leader's position.

Conducting an initial survey

How can you know which of the "core areas" is going to require your attention first of all? Look to the context, because it alone will determine which of the "core areas" you need to attend to first in your transition. You need to find out for yourself what the context requires. Only you should gather the data, and make sense of it. You will shape your early leadership of the organisation by how you do this.

How can you investigate the context? Our suggestion is simple:

1 Start a process of enquiry with selected people in the organisation (and sometimes outside it).

2 Identify who you need to talk to in the organisation, from different levels and functions.

3 Conduct as systematic a survey of opinions as you can afford, in the time you have.

4 Enquire, day-in, day-out, and with increasing thoroughness, into the matters which are of interest to the people you are interviewing, whether or not these fall neatly into the "Core Areas."

Here are three questions to ask others that will yield gold dust as you conduct your enquiry into context:

- How does the organisation support you to do a good job? Be specific.

- What needs changing for you to be more fulfilled at work?

- What would you like *me* to do?

Tips for success

1 Do not lead your interviewees. Let them lead *you* to what they see as important. You may or may not share their sense of importance.

2 What you want to learn is how they think and how they see their organisation. As you enquire, you will probably go through periods of what seem like crystal-clear clarity. Those are wonderful. But beware! Just around the corner you will encounter periods when you are in the deepest of dark fogs. But take courage! Just around the corner will be periods of crystal-clear clarity. Investigating context is akin to the waves of culture-shock people experience when they live in very different cultures than their own. At times, they think they really understand how people think, and then at others they do not think they understand anything at all!

3 We recommend that you employ the Journaling and Freefall tools, also to be found in this section, to record what you are finding and thinking. The broader and more incisive your thinking at the start of your transition, the more likely you will be able to bring fresh and helpful insights and questions to your colleagues. The time will quickly come when you are no longer fresh. Remember: you can only be new once. Take advantage of it while you still are.

Spotting your priority issues to tackle

Once you have done your survey, we suggest that you take an hour or two off to do some analysis. These are the four steps:

1 Draw out on a flipchart the diagram overleaf. Make sure that there is plenty of space around the four ovals.

2 Write out on separate Post-its the issues which you will need to ensure are tackled in the forthcoming 12–18 months. Do not worry if the number of Post-it's is large or small. Just write what you believe to be the case.

3 Now select place the Post-its where you think they most obviously belong on the flipchart. Most will have an obvious place

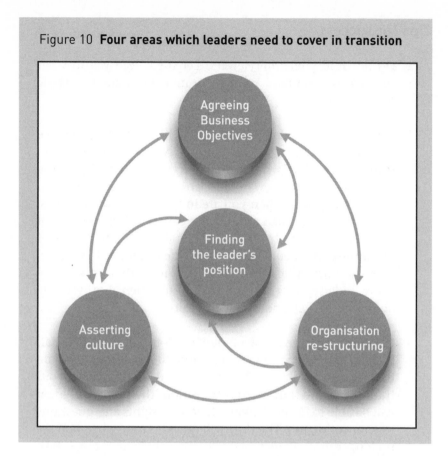

Figure 10 **Four areas which leaders need to cover in transition**

attached to one of the ovals. In some cases, the decision will not be so clear and you will need to reflect where the Post-it fits best. In some cases, the Post-it will fall outside the Core Areas and should be placed on the periphery of the flipchart.

4 Now stand back and notice what you see. Which of the Core Areas is the most densely covered in Post-it's? Which of the Core Areas feels most pressing? Which of the Core Areas is the "show-stopper"? (If you don't get that one right, everything else may go pear-shaped.)

5 Now list the two or three "hills you must climb" in your transition if you are to be ready to tackle the Core Area(s) you have decided will be critical in the next 12–18 months?

Having done this task, you will know what you need to do in transition to be ready to tackle the Core Areas. These will need your attention most urgently if you are to successfully lead this organisation.

Validating your conclusions

Despite the rigour of your analysis and the thoroughness of your survey, you may still have missed significant themes and data about the context. Check your emerging conclusions with your colleague's team and the team you lead. When you are confident that your choice is solid, let the people in your organisation know what your initial priorities will be and why. Let them know your thinking. This will tell them what sort of person you are, what matters to you most and where you intend to prioritise. They will need to know these things if they are going to decide to follow you. They will almost always take this decision during the transition phase.

Designing and doing experiments

Henry Ford once said, "You can't build a reputation on what you're going to do." As one of the earliest champions of affordable motor cars for the thousands of Americans enjoying new wealth and wanting greater mobility, Henry Ford understood that he would only have one chance to satisfy that need. If this exciting but new fangled machine called a motor car didn't deliver all it promised, he would have a lot of angry and disappointed people who would be unlikely to buy another one. He had to keep what he did simple (any colour you like so long as it's black) and deliver it at a price people would pay. Henry Ford's vision of mobile Americans was responsible for some of the most radical and pioneering engineering in the manufacture of motor cars. The rest is history.

We could see what Henry Ford did as a colossal experiment: matching opportunity with innovation to bring about something no one had seen before. On a different scale this is also how experiments work for you personally as you set about adapting your own leadership to the context in which you arrive. We define experiments as:

A chosen set of actions designed by you to expand your understanding and practice of how you operate.

Using NOW for change

Experiments are essential in transitions because they give you permission to try out things you have not done before and in doing so to access new information about yourself. They rest on the idea that change can only happen in the present – the past has gone and the future is yet to happen so acting differently in either time zone is impossible. When we do dwell on the past as a place for change our focus is likely to be on the regrets of lost opportunity or the review of what *has* worked. Neither of these kinds of reflection directly change much about where we are now, although reflection helps us to learn what has worked and what hasn't, which might translate into different choices for the present and future. When we choose the future for our focus, we engage in wishful thinking and hopeful dreaming: both can be inspiring but neither in themselves produce change. So if you can't build a reputation on what you're *going* to do –what's left? The present – NOW.

Experiments are the way you create "living knowledge" about yourself; they update you with who you are NOW in this role at this time of your life. Much of what you will know about yourself is familiar. By now, you know a good deal about how you typically like to act in certain situations. Bringing yourself up to date with yourself and not relying on familiar and maybe even ancient knowledge about yourself, is what experiments can help you to do. And once your knowledge is up to date you are far better equipped to make wise choices and decisions about what to change about yourself and what to maintain as you are. Just as Henry Ford matched opportunity with innovation, so too will you as you design your experiments. For you the opportunity is a new leadership role: the innovation will be how you exploit your context to creatively find ways to change.

Here's how to design experiments

1. The discovery goal

Describe what you want to find out about yourself – called a discovery goal. The discipline of a succinct statement of your goal will sharpen the experiment and the focus you take towards yourself. Aim to complete the sentence, "What I want to discover about myself is ...." Some possible ends to it could be:

- How I can be more collaborative?
- How I can make myself more accessible to my peers?
- What impact I have when I speak less.
- What to say when I don't know the answer?

2. Evoke some anticipation or risk

- To deliberately learn something new about yourself involves stretching yourself beyond your immediate comfort zone. The risk you take doesn't need to be huge, in fact this is not the time to test your inner dare devil. But it does need to invoke some nervousness or even mild fear when you imagine yourself actually doing the tasks you set yourself.

- Name the risk or fear contained in your discovery goal. Almost always the real risk will be to some aspect of your self-image or self-control. Occasionally your goal might involve a business risk, but taking business risks still all come back eventually to questions of personal reputation or competence.

For instance, if your Discovery Goal was "How can I be more collaborative?" You might decide that what you will do is to hand over some decision making to your team. The risk will be that you have to go along with decisions you don't like; but the *real* risk is that if they don't work you will get associated with failure (and equally if they *do* work you may not get the kudos!). Or the risk is that people will not see you out in front leading in the way they know and the *real* risk is they will see you as indecisive. Both these examples might hold small business risks but they hold far larger risks to self-image.

3. Grading or scaling

- You can design your experiment in several parts. For instance, you might want to start by choosing a low risk action and gradually scale up using different people and situations to discover how you can stretch what you know of yourself in such situations. Remember, one person's high risk is another person's safety zone.

- To continue with the example above, you might decide to begin collaborating differently with a colleague; you may decide to involve him more actively in working out a plan you know will involve several people in his department. A low risk start. Then you decide that once the outline of the plan has been decided you will open up the detailed planning to everyone who is to be involved in its implementation. And you decide you will leave it to them to make the final decision as to what that plan looks like. The greater risk here is the readiness to trust others to know what needs to happen: and your fear is that the trust may be misplaced and you will be let down.

4. Find support

- All risk and change is easier to undertake if we are supported well. Decide what kind of support you need to operate outside your comfort zone. It may be time, someone else, information, a good massage, exercise, getting away from it all for a few hours, a mentor, peace and quiet, etc, etc. All these – and others – are supports which can boost courage and determination to step into the new. You will need to find your own.

5. Record your discovery

- New awareness and knowledge of yourself can be fleeting. Make sure you capture what you are finding out by Journaling and Freefall Writing.

Watchpoints for success

✓ Having designed your experiment, make sure you carry it out. Talking about change, changes nothing.

✓ If you are not sure what your discovery goal might be, ask a few other people who see enough of how you operate to give you some ideas. This in itself is an experiment full of plenty of risk for some people!

✓ Take time to reflect on what you find out about yourself. Just taking action, without making sense of the action and its consequences, risks wasting the action.

Silencing the Inner Critic: Freefall writing

In the first section on the myths of transition we described how common it is for people arriving in a new role to need to appear confident, competent and fully in charge. And how wide of the mark this usually is in reality. Sustaining this kind of gap – between how we feel and how we appear – is tough when you are under constant scrutiny by others also wanting to understand what you are like and how to work with you.

Feelings and appearance are out of synch

One reason why our behaviour often doesn't reflect how we feel is the belief that we shouldn't feel as we do. Even though rationally we know it is normal to feel nervous, maybe even terrified, when faced with the demands of delivering hugely stretching goals, we still manage to believe that this is "just me"; nobody else feels like this. And so we work hard to look cool, collected and fully in control. Over time the gap between how we feel and how we operate can become too much and the strain shows up in a variety of ways: not sleeping well; making poor decisions; short temper; concentration becomes difficult etc. You may already have had this kind of experience when you have been under pressure in past roles.

The ever present Inner Critic

These inner messages about how we *should* behave, despite feeling quite the opposite, are often called our Inner Critic or Inner Fascist. This is your silent but persistent internal voice that only you can hear which says, "I should be able to handle this with no trouble – after all everyone else is." Or "I'd better make sure I know exactly what they are talking about here – they did hire me to sort this out." Or "How come it's only me that thinks this situation is a mess? Nobody else seems worried. Must be me."

One of the most useful ways you can support yourself through transition is to find ways to dilute the corrosive power of your Inner Critic. Not only does it undermine you, but it also prevents you from responding well to current experience. If you know the experiences described here, then probably your Inner Critic is alive and far too well for your own good. When you find your confidence particularly low, or you feel dispirited at how you are coping, pick yourself up with a session of Freefall Writing. You can use this in combination with Journaling for an even more powerful tool.

What it is

This is a way of capturing and describing your experience which silences your Inner Critic. It is a form of writing that cuts out logic, analysis and evaluation – often invitations to the Inner Critic – and can reveal to you new insights about your experience and uncensored thoughts about yourself. It is a personal way to validate and approve what is going on as you make the transition into this role. For some people, just trying this out will seem like a huge experiment!

Here's how to do it

1 Write whatever comes into your head – it doesn't have to make sense – ramblings are fine.

2 Keep your pen moving and on the paper at all times – even writing "I don't know what to write" keeps your pen moving.

3 Nothing is off limits – write whatever comes into your head, including wild or dangerous thoughts.

4 Write for ten minutes then stop wherever you are.

5 Repeat as often as is helpful.

6 From time to time go back over what you have written and notice

   • Persistent themes. Are there certain situations/people/issues which keep recurring?
   • How has what you are writing about changed recently compared with when you began? What does this tell you about you and your transition?

Watchpoints for success

✓ Don't cross out or edit as you go – you inhibit the flow if you do.

✓ Ignore spelling, grammar and punctuation – it's not an essay and nobody will mark it.

✓ Don't get logical – what you write doesn't have to "make sense." Get several writings done before you look back and see whether there is any sense to be made.

Using a journal

The French existential writer, Albert Camus, had this to say about change:

> Great ideas come into the world as gently as doves. Perhaps then if we listen attentively we shall hear, amid the uproar of empires and nations, a faint flutter of wings, the gentle stirring of life and hope. Some will say this hope lies in a nation, others, in a man or woman. I believe rather that it is awakened, revived, nourished by millions of solitary individuals whose deeds and works every day negate frontiers.

What he is pointing out in the wonderful language of a talented writer, is that what each of us does every day is what makes for change. Most likely, some or all of your brief in this role will be to bring about change in some part of your organisation. As you arrive one of the most important things you can do is to get an accurate fix fairly quickly on the context in which you are working. You will be bombarded with information – both explicitly and through your own observations – of what this context is about and how it feels and operates. How do you harvest this bounty of information so that you collect and retain the most striking nuggets for later use?

What you see, hear and experience in your early weeks will be fresh, vivid, surprising, maybe sometimes disappointing, but all grist to the mill of really appreciating how your organisation works – and how you are adapting to it. You can only be new once and only see with the special focus of new eyes once, so capturing the treasure trove of what is happening is too valuable to lose. Journaling offers a way to "awaken, revive and nourish" your thoughts, conclusions, insights and ideas about how you are and how you want to operate. Leaders who are strongly action driven with less of a reflective preference, usually look at us with astonishment when we suggest they try this. When they give it a go, many are surprised at the value they get from pausing to draw their thinking into one place. If you are such a leader, we'd encourage you to get beyond your astonishment (if you have even made it this far) and also give this a go.

Here's how to do it

1   Set up a new file on your computer or use a small notebook if you prefer to hand write.

2   Find a time each day (ideally) when you make short notes about what is standing out for you in your experience at the moment. Some people use commuting time to jot down their notes, others as a wind down to the day once they are home. Airplanes and airports are also great places to take some time to yourself and complete your journal. You can just write (see the earlier exercise on Freefall Writing) or use the following headings to help guide your writings:

Observation Notes. – as concrete and detailed accounts of what you see, hear and feel about the events you are engaged in. Include responses to what you do, as well as any feedback you receive, and any changes you make to your actions.

Ideas/Insight Notes. These are hunches, bright ideas or critical observations on what you are doing. They may become mini explanations about how you or the business are operating which you might want to test out as you meet and talk with other people.

Personal Notes. These are feeling statements about your work, the people you are working with, your doubts, anxieties and pleasures. Having your feelings out on paper will stimulate your creativity and ideas. Personal notes are also a way for you to get to know yourself better in this phase of your role.

Making sense of your notes

So that the value of what you are noticing and recording is not lost, look over them from time to time – say once a month – and see what themes are emerging about:

- The organisation, its culture, your role and your understanding so far of how these come together.
- You, your leadership and how you are handling your transition.
- Others, their impact on you and how you are dealing with them.

- Evaluations: how you are getting on with changes you are making in your own style, your operational role.

People who regularly keep journals often say how useful their writings are long after the event they are capturing. It's as though the reflection comes before it's time and matures into action or application at a later date.

Watchpoints for success

✓ A little and often works best.

✓ Keep it confidential – you are writing for *you* and nobody else. We all write differently if we know we are writing for others. Keep hard copy journals safe from accidental loss.

✓ Pictures, diagrams, doodles and scribbles are just as useful and valid in a journal as beautiful prose.

"Eavesdropping": A fast route to feedback

The origins of the word "gossip" lie in early medieval history. It was customary then for the mother of a newborn child to invite to her bedside a group of close friends and others who she hoped would be influential in her child's life. The group would meet, with the baby's crib in their midst, and talk about the new arrival. They would describe the life they saw the child leading, the hopes they held for her and what they thought they would personally contribute to her life. They believed that, by talking about the baby's future, literally over the baby's head with the baby "eavesdropping," they helped her play a part in shaping her life. This group of well-wishers was called a "gossip."

Today of course we have modified the meaning of "gossip" into something quite different: no longer a collection of well-wishers helping to speak a new future into existence but something frivolous, usually done by women and often with a slightly malicious edge to it. Eavesdropping is a form of feedback which very much draws on the original medieval meaning of "gossip" for its purpose and intent.

Why we need feedback

Feedback is crucial to our understanding of ourselves. Without it we run the risk of believing our own press unchecked by the editing of others. Feedback provides the information which ensures the picture we have of ourselves – our identity – can flex and adapt to changing circumstances. Feedback helps free us from self-defeating patterns of interaction and belief. But feedback also opens up anxiety about what I will hear and how to handle it. We are innately self-protecting of who we are and why we act the way we do. The tendency to avoid or defend how we are to others is triggered quickly when we hear information about ourselves which contradicts how we think we are. In the flurry of explanations which feedback can provoke in the listener, is often lost the quietness which can allow us to really hear and absorb what is said so that we can sort out what is valuable and what can be discarded.

But remember that what you do with feedback is a choice. Often we confuse the feedback (information) with the automatic assumption that it is information we should act upon. Not true. Feedback is like any other information: it can support good action if it is well considered, but not all information is automatically conducive to good action. Take your time to decide what YOU want to do with the feedback you get about yourself. Sometimes feedback tells you more about the giver than it may about you.

For you as a new leader, getting to hear quickly how you are coming across and the impact you are having is crucial as part of knowing where and what to adjust in your behaviour and approach. Knowing more about these areas of performance is central to building confidence and competence, yet can be hard to get in some organisations where feedback is not a well established mechanism for learning and performance improvement.

Eavesdropping is a technique for giving and getting feedback that gives the receiver the time and space to hear what is said without any need for a response. And it gives the feedback sayers the chance to "speak over the head of the baby" without interruption. The outcome, whenever we have used this approach, has always been described as invaluable and one of the best experiences of feedback. See what you think.

Here's how to do it

1 Bring together a group of people – maybe your team, or it could be a more random group whose views interest you – and explain the purpose and method of eavesdropping. If you are using your team, you could extend this to include everyone, not only you.

2 One person, who will be the subject of feedback, moves to a corner of the room or somewhere out of line of sight of the rest of the group. Really separating from the group is important. It frees up the feedback givers to engage more freely (see below) and also frees the subject of the feedback to listen well freed from the pressure to engage in what is being said.

3 The group now begins a discussion about the focussed individual which works through the following three questions:

   a) What is [xxx] doing which is having a positive impact on ... (choose the focus, eg the team, the organisation, his boss, the change agenda etc)?
   b) What would we recommend that he changes to be even more effective?
   c) What support can we offer him to do so?

Allow about 15–20 minutes for this discussion.

4 The individual listening to the feedback can take notes, simply sit and hear it, but cannot interrupt and ask questions while the group is discussing him.

5 After the time is up, the feedback subject can ask any questions to better understand what was meant, but there is no discussion or challenge to what has been said.

6 If others are having a go, repeat the process with each member of the group.

7 Once everyone has been the subject of an eavesdropping, take ten minutes for individual reflection. Use this time to clarify for yourself what stands out and what you intend to act on – if anything. Remember to take up any of the specific offers of help that were offered in 3c above.

8 Take turns going around the group and hear from each person. Making public commitments to change can make the change more likely to happen.

Watchpoints of success

✓ This can be an exposing process if not handled well. Use a facilitator or someone who can keep the conversation on track and support the contributors to be open and constructive.

✓ Set the context and purpose for this approach very clearly. Get agreements to confidentiality.

✓ Aim for a balance in the feedback. Most organisations are so problem or issues-oriented that it comes through in feedback too. Make sure people provide good news about you as well as what they would like you to change.

Story Circles: Bringing experience to life

Stories are central to expressing ourselves and letting other people know who we are and what we are experiencing. So how does storytelling contribute to managing a successful transition? We have described in section 4 how the willingness to learn is central to moving successfully into a new role: learning about yourself, about others around you and making sense of the context. The Reciprocity tension balances the need for you to bring to the present situation the value of your experience; and also the readiness to learn from others who may have more knowledge of what is really going on and how things really work around here than you do.

Dan McAdams writes about how we use stories to tell ourselves and others who we are; a kind of ongoing explanation of who we are becoming as we live our lives and do our work. He says:

> Human beings are storytellers by nature. In many guises, as folktale, legend, myth, epic, history, motion picture and television programme, the story appears in every known human culture. The story is a natural package for organising many different kinds of information. Storytelling appears to be a fundamental way of expressing ourselves and our world to others. Think of the last time you tried to explain something really important about yourself to another person. Chances are you accomplished this task by telling a story ... Indeed much of what passes for everyday conversation among people is storytelling of one form or another.

If stories are "the natural package for organising many different kinds of information," this tool provides you with a way to sort through the tumult of information about your new organisation, your team or other significant topics you want to explore and understand better. The method we offer here is called a Story Circle.

Story Circles offer:

- A way for you to engage with both ends of the Reciprocity tension.

- A means to break the ice with your team and get to know more about them when you arrive.

- An approach and a process which itself highlights your willingness to be open about yourself.

In our work with new leaders we frequently use Story Circles as an engaging way to:

- Help people get to know each other quickly in the context of a new role.

- Share personal and often formative experiences of success-fully handling transitions.

- Connect their past experience of other transitions with what is happening currently.

- Validate leaders' already-held transition skills as a way of building confidence.

Here's how to do it

1   Sit in a circle or round a table. Make it so everyone can see everyone else if at all possible. To do this will take the following times:

   a) Set up and introductions: 5 minutes
   b) Storytelling: 3 minutes per person
   c) Theme identifying: 5–10 minutes
   d) Summarising: 5 minutes

2   One person – ideally you – acts as the facilitator or manager of the circle. If you are with a group who doesn't know each other, introduce yourself; then moving clockwise, each person states their name and gives a *very brief* introduction of themselves (name and where from).

3   Be aware of how much time you have for the whole Story Circle process (see above) and let everyone know how long this will take.

4   Decide on the number of minutes for each story; we suggest three minutes. Time-keeping is important: pass a watch around the circle so that the person on the right of the storyteller keeps time for him, then the person who has just told a story keeps time for the person on his left etc, moving round the circle.

5   If there is to be a theme for the stories, the facilitator explains the theme and answers any questions about that theme or about the process itself. It helps to have the theme clearly expressed so there is no confusion as to what you are asking people to tell their story about. The ways we would express the theme for the areas described above are:

   • Tell a story about a time which stands out for you when you went through a transition. The story can be work based or personally based.
   • Tell a story about a time when you know you handled a significant transition well. Include what you did that you believe helped your success
   • Tell a story about a transition you have come through which seems to connect with what is happening now. You can relate it to personal experience, to organisation issues or others which seem important to you.
   • Tell a story from your experience of transition, which illustrates the key areas that helped you come through it.

6   The facilitator calls for the first story. Anyone may begin and you move clockwise round the group.

7   Any person may pass when their time comes. People who pass will have a chance at the end of the circle to tell a story.

8   The stories you tell should be *stories*, not political theories, general histories or your opinion on the theme, or your opportunity to lecture. A story is just that; it is told without needing explanations.

9   The essence of story telling is the listening. Listening is more important than talking. Don't spend time thinking of what your story will be; just actively listen to the stories. Trust that the circle will bring you a story. If several stories come to you as you are listening, go for the one that is the "deepest," that you feel comfortable telling.

10   Do not take notes as stories are being told. Concentrate on listening.

11   Silence is OK; in fact it is good. As the stories pass around the circle it is OK for there to be silence after one story is complete and before the next person begins. This gives that person, and the circle, time to reflect on the story they just heard, and it gives the next person time to land on his/her story, or decide to pass without pressure.

12   You don't have to agree with someone's story; more important is to notice how different it may be from your experience. It doesn't need agreement or disagreement.

13   As you move around the group, there is no "cross circle" talk, questions or commenting on the story just told. Make sure anyone who passed has a chance to tell their story, and when everyone has done so, invite questions, comments and dialogue.

14   This is the point at which people can describe any themes that have emerged from the collection of stories they have just listened to.

15   Surfacing themes is a useful way of highlighting the commonalities or differences of experience – both are useful for learning from. Finally, if you have time for more than one circle of stories, begin the process all over again, with a related but different topic.

Authors' note: With acknowledgements to Theresa Holden, Leadership for a Changing World Project (Wagner Graduate School of Public Service, New York University) and Managing Director, Junebug Productions/The Color Line Project/TH@Holdenarts.org

We would also like to thank Geoff Mead of Hermes Consulting who is a master storyteller himself and has contributed generously to our understanding of how stories can be used in organisations.

Watch points for success

✓ A Story Circle takes time: don't try and squeeze it into less time than it deserves.

✓ Keep to the "rules": they really do help a Story Circle to work successfully.

✓ Have the topic for the circle very clearly written up where everyone can see it – keep it succinct.

Tensions: Expanding the choices to act and resolving business contradictions

Section 3 was devoted entirely to describing and exploring 8 Tensions which are at work during leadership transitions. These first emerged in Richard Elsner's research with Gilles Amado in 2003–2004. They have been validated in the work of The Turning Point in the years since then. Many leaders have found that these tensions are true; that is, they are an accurate way of representing the experience they have. The tensions get to the heart of the choices that leaders need to make in transition and of the ingrained preferences they start from.

As you will see if you complete the Personal Style Questionnaire in the Appendix, you will discover your preference for eight of the sixteen poles in the 8 Tensions (for example, you may have a preference for the Developing Bonds pole, as opposed to the Keeping Distance pole, in the Relationship tension). To have a preference is to be most at home in a pole, to have most knowledge of it and to have the greatest range of responses from within it. So, if Developing Bonds was your preference, we might expect you to be used to and competent at

- being relaxed with others

- being open with others

- creating trust with others

- sharing your thoughts with others.

And so on …

Preferring one pole and what that means

Having a preference for one pole means that the other pole is less well developed, and that you have less knowledge of it. Does this matter? It may, depending on the context which you are in. Most leaders in transition discover that the new context they are in demands that they demonstrate a real comfort in some of the behaviours from their less developed pole. This means that they need to develop into that pole, or they may be unable to rise to the demands of the context. When that happens, difficulties usually arrive on the scene for the leader and his transition. So in the case of the Relationship tension mentioned above, your less developed pole would be "Keeping Distance." To develop that pole, you would need to become more used to and competent at, for example:

- setting firm boundaries

- insisting on your own privacy

- defining and allocating tasks

- communicating priorities.

And so on ...

Putting the opposite pole into practice

Does that sound easy to do? It might in the abstract, but ask anyone around you who has a strong preference for "Developing Bonds" and they will tell you that they will find the typical behaviours of "Keeping Distance" difficult to do, and also to develop more fluency with. And, of course, this applies vice versa to those people who are most at home with "Keeping Distance." These less-developed behaviours will be difficult to undertake, and even scary. Most of us are more estranged from our less preferred poles than we like to think. We set ourselves up as one or the other, and then build our identity around one pole as a source of pride. "I am the kind of person who is good at developing bonds. That is who I am. Keeping Distance is not my thing." That is how we have learnt to be, normally subconsciously, and we tend to stick rigidly to that single identity. We fear that if we were to develop into the other pole that we would undermine ourselves. We see our identity as dependent on us choosing between one or the other. The more I am one pole, the stronger my identity will be, or so we think.

Limits to using one pole

That thinking does not serve us well as leaders in transition. It would do if only we were back in the contexts we knew and have become expert at navigating. But in the new, unfamiliar and stretching contexts we must inhabit as leaders in transition, this thinking can be our undoing. If we stick to one pole in each of the 8 Tensions, we will be more limited and less flexible than we need to be. In fact, we will be slightly more than half the person we need to be to succeed. Your transition may depend on it.

Three tensions come to the fore frequently at the beginning

In practice, you will find that you need to develop yourself in a limited number (usually two or three) tensions at any one point in time. Typically, at the beginning of a transition, leaders experience the need to develop their competence in the following tensions:

- Mission
- Relationship
- Pace of Change

This is not always the case, but frequently so. As the leader's transition progresses, he often finds that one or other of the remaining tensions (Reciprocity, Decision-making, Faith, Loyalty and Goal Orientation) comes into focus and requires attention. Once again, the order will vary from leader to leader; what seems usual is that a selection of the tensions imposes itself on the leader, due to how his preferences and the needs of the context inter-act. As a rule, the leader will need to develop the pole which the context demands he develop. For example, to take the Relationship tension again, a leader with a strong preference for "Developing Bonds" will need to develop "Keeping Distance" if the context calls for:

- greater focus on results
- a more performance-oriented culture

- more freedom of manoeuvre for the leader
- a lack of any risk of "taking sides" in existing conflicts.

And so on …

Whether or not the leader chooses to develop his competence in his less developed poles is his choice.

How can one develop one's less developed pole?

The process for developing into a less-developed pole contains five steps. Within each step, there are activities and questions. Going through the five steps only once will not get you anywhere fast. What you are attempting to do here is to re-learn a set of behaviours which you have consciously or unconsciously neglected, as you have made choices over many years about who you are or want to be. This is not easy work, but it is achievable. It does not happen overnight. It takes repeated experiments at practising the less familiar behaviours, making fumbled attempts, learning a little more each time, and slowly broadening your range of available behaviours as a result. By so doing, you will fill out as a leader, and as a person. The two are of course inseparable, even if we often sometimes like to think that we can exist in the role of the leader independently of the person inside sustaining the role.

The five-step pathway to developing the less developed pole is:

1. Identify your preference

You will find that the Personal Style Questionnaire in the Appendix will help you identify your preference within each of the tensions. Your preference is the pole in which you have the most strongly developed competence. Most people are generally unsurprised by the questionnaire results. They know which pole they are most at home in – and they also know which pole they struggle with. When we acquaint leaders with the 8 Tensions for the first time, they often respond, "Yes, I have been working on *that* one for years – and without much success" or, "This tension is *so* familiar to me" or, "These two poles are constantly in flux for me."

The greater the matching of intensity between the poles, the easier it is for you to switch flexibly from behaviours typical of one pole to those typical of the other. To use the example of the Relationship tension we were discussing above, the greater the matching of your competence between "Developing Bonds" and "Keeping Distance," the more you will be able to switch between the two behaviour modes.

2. Give yourself some praise for your preference

When we identify with one pole rather than the other (which most people do 80 percent of the time), something strange happens after a while. Rather than get more and more positive benefits from our preferred pole (for example, lots of trust, understanding and willingness to engage from the "Developing Bonds" pole), we start to get increasing amounts of negative stuff. For example, from too much identification with "Developing Bonds," we will start to harvest downsides like a loss of focus on performance, a sense of being hemmed in as a leader and of being pushed and pulled between opposing camps. These things are unpleasant and create dissatisfaction in us. We want to get out of this place, but do not know exactly where to go. The other pole looks attractive, but what about all those things you fear about that pole, if one identified too much with it? For example, if one switched to "Keeping Distance," what about the downsides of resistance to change, the sense of mistrust and aloofness and the feelings people have of not being heard? Before we can address those, we have another task first.

Our next task is to remember how useful our preferred pole has been to us. Take some time to give that pole its due. Let it bask in the sun of your appreciation for a while. Although you can see that you have overdone it with that pole, and some negative results have ensued, you can't blame the pole for that. Remember the benefits the pole has brought you. If you are thinking about "Developing Bonds" in the Relationship tension, think about the trusting relationships you have created, the sense of community you have engendered, and the easy access you have had to people. Really take time to visualise those benefits which have accrued to you. If it helps to remember them, write them down.

3. Now get to know the benefits of the other pole

Although you may feel that the other pole is "not you," you are wrong there. It is "you" all right, even if it is less pronounced in you than your preferred pole. You started out in life with less of a leaning towards this pole, and you discovered that you were less competent in it. In fact, you may have felt quite awkward when trying to act out this pole, and you may have felt embarrassment and even humiliation as you showed up as incompetent here. What did you do with those feelings? You may have turned those feelings of unhappiness about you "in general" into unhappiness toward that pole in particular. You may have created deep feelings of dislike and fear towards the pole, which take time to overcome.

So to take our example of the Relationship tension, if you found yourself to be incompetent in "Keeping Distance," you may have learnt to shun and rubbish behaviours of distance exhibited by yourself or others. "Keeping Distance" really became a bit of a bogeyman for you, and you decided that it was the opposite of who you really are, the "Developing Bonds" person. That choice, while understandable at the time, may (if you cannot undo it now) hold you back from fulfilling the leadership potential you have. Slowly but surely, you need to reacquaint yourself with the positive results that come from "Keeping Distance." You will remember that we listed these as:

- greater focus on results
- a more performance-oriented culture
- more freedom of manoeuvre for the leader
- a lack of any risk of "taking sides" in existing conflicts.

These are far from negligible. Indeed, every leader needs to be able to engender them. Without enough of these, all the "Developing Bonds" in the world will not deliver the success you need as the leader.

Really weigh up those benefits. Are you convinced that they are essential to your success? Do you really need them? Once you have assured yourself that you need them, you are ready for the next exploration.

4. Go diving into your fears about the other pole

Your fears about what will happen if (and when) it "takes over" are what have probably held you back from this pole, because you may fear that it will take over as much as your preferred one has to date. You may not yet trust yourself to establish a reasonable balance between the two, a balance that you can adjust from time to time to deal with changing circumstances. In fact, you may fear change itself because it threatens to brush to one side the identity you have fought so hard to make for yourself. So tackling those fears about the other pole may loosen up your reluctance to acquire a more flexible identity. Could you confront your fears about "Keeping Distance" (assuming that you were strong in "Developing Bonds")? Remember that we said those might include:

- resistance to change
- the sense of mistrust and aloofness
- the feelings people have of not being heard.

These are not attractive, are they? They are precisely what the people "not like you," your professional opposites, tend to create, aren't they? You definitely do not want to be like them. But ask yourself, why do those people tend to get those negative results (which we can assume they do not want either)? They get them because they over-do "Keeping Distance" and do not develop "Developing Bonds" enough. They are the reverse mirror image of yourself.

So, how can you get the positive results of "Keeping Distance" (which are desirable), without all those negative downsides we have just listed? You can get them by accepting that "Keeping Distance" is part of yourself, and by refusing to ever make "Keeping Distance" your exclusive play, as you have perhaps made "Developing Bonds" to date. You can get them by loosening up the hold which "Developing Bonds" has had on you, and becoming a flexible, ambidextrous person in the Relationship tension. By doing that you will also avoid the downsides you have been harvesting with too much emphasis on your preferred pole: We listed these as

- a loss of focus on performance
- a sense of being hemmed in as a leader, and of
- being pushed and pulled between opposing camps.

You can do this by starting on the path to experimentation.

5. Build up a battery of experiments to enhance the other pole

So by now you know which pole you need to develop, what positive results you can expect to get from doing that and what negative results you can avoid. All you need to do is go out there and experiment. Simple, no? No! Experimenting is a tough, long road, which does not have iron-cast guarantees of success attached to it. It requires patience, endurance and quite a lot of humility. But we know of no other way for adults to change themselves at work.

For example, if you were wishing to strengthen your "Developing Bonds" pole, you might experiment with some of the following behaviours:

- Inquire without judgement into your own and others' behaviour.
- Identify to whom others have loyalties, and respect these as you engage.

- Work to internally separate well and respectfully from your previous organisation.
- At an appropriate time, reveal to others critical experiences which have shaped your way of leading and being, and invite others to do the same.
- Acknowledge the existing structure and leadership, and give it due credit for past achievements, before beginning to change these.
- Connect systematically with all the different groups in the organisation, making sure each group feels heard and understood.

Those are examples. You will be able to create your own list to suit the needs of your own context.

For guidance on the process of experimentation, see Designing and Doing Experiments starting on p. 175.

Conclusion:
Leaning into the slope –
Thriving on transitions

Our own journey of delving into the turbulent times of transition has led to some surprising discoveries and confirmed strongly a few existing hunches about what it takes to handle this time with grace, energy and open eyes. Let us try to wrap up our main learning so far.

Just tell me what to do

When we begin working with new in-post leaders, they typically want the summary version and main action points: just tell me the key things I need to do, they ask. So this is what we tell them:

> To move through the early months of your new role as successfully as possible, working as effectively as you can as a leader and catalyst of change, you will need to:
>
> • Have the confidence to hold uncertainty.
> • Be open enough to change personally.
> • Demand and use appropriate support.
> • Work the transition as a process not an event.

We get a whole range of reactions to this list: surprise, puzzlement, relief, interest, disagreement, challenge, questions. Rarely indifference. So in this final section we'd like to distil what each of these is about, so we leave you with food for further thought, stimulate you into using all or some of what we are suggesting and prompt you to keep your eyes open and looking for the unique, new experiences of the transition you are in or about to start.

The confidence to hold uncertainty

- This is the most paradoxical outcome of our research. Human beings are inherently *not* confident with uncertainty. We invest great effort in pinning down actions, measuring outcomes, slicing our time into tighter and tighter segments, securing systems, checking up, reviewing against milestones and all so that we can always know – feel confident – of where events have been and the direction where they are moving. We have created regulatory bodies who come along behind whole industries to check that they are really operating as they say. We truly leave little to chance. Yet in the face of all this, we know too that how actions and events will turn out is not always even close to what we hoped for and planned. The new leader has to reckon with this paradox from day one.

- Leaders in transition also have to hold uncertainty about themselves – probably the hardest place of all to remain uncertain. Transitions have the scope, if you allow them, to bring about personal change by deepening your skills and capabilities and surfacing aspects of yourself that you may not have known about. They can bring you more fully into yourself. But for that to happen leaders have to tolerate the turbulence that takes place in shifting identity – who you know yourself to be – towards who you might become.

- New leaders are not only experiencing the transition for themselves – those they join will also be doing so. They may have been facing uncertainty following the exit of a loved or respected leader; they may be jubilant at seeing the back of a tyrant; for sure they will be in the space between departing and arriving. Smart and sensitive arriving leaders will appreciate the situation is similar but different for those around him and work to keep himself aware of where others are in relation to him.

- The Arabic phrase "Trust in Allah and tether your camel" sums up the paradox of confidently holding uncertainty. It would be foolish to venture into the desert without trusting in Allah to see you through safely. But if at night you were to leave all the responsibility to Allah and leave your camel untethered you would be equally foolish. Life is uncertain but you can take steps to make it less so without pretending those steps will always work out as you planned.

The openness to personal change

- To be open to changing yourself means to start by knowing something about who you are, what makes you tick and how you operate. It means being able to say what matters to you, what you believe in and why you hold those beliefs. In other words to have a reasonable level of self-knowledge and understanding. When you are interested in who you are and curious about how you come to be who you are, it's likely that you will be open and even excited to use your transition as a crash course in deepening that interest. Leaders who realised that self-knowing was a constant process were able to make more deliberate choices of what to reveal of themselves and what to keep hidden. It enabled them to have increased options in choosing how they acted, including experimenting deliberately with new and different modes of behaviour.

- Having a sounder grasp on the reality of who you are increases versatility which in turn increases the scope for choice of action – both personally and organisationally. Confidence too is often linked to being able to exercise control over choices that matter to you.

- Expanding how you know yourself is valuable because the leader seemed more "human" and that shifted the relationship with the team and others to a stronger and more open one. It is also the basis for building trust. Trust is not a thing, it's a feature which is developed over time between people who are prepared to risk revealing aspects of themselves and to encourage others to invest in similar ways.

Demand and use appropriate support

- Support is not a trivial need at times of personal change. We found that leaders who believed in "toughing out" the early months of their transition were less credible to others and struggled personally to get their feet under the table. Getting the right support is as central to your success as choosing the best people or developing the right strategy. Calling on inner and outer resources to sustain yourself through the early weeks of arriving in a new role is demanding stuff. Negotiating for appropriate support from your boss and team is an action that releases you from the pressure to go it alone and signals a proactivity to your own transition management.

- New situations are inherently uncertain: responding to them involves taking risks of the right kind and at the right time. Taking a risk asks you to have some degree of confidence that what you are doing will probably yield the result you want. So how do you generate confidence? Confidence can be generated through a range of support mechanisms.

- Support means something different for everyone. Work out what support looks like to you and ruthlessly set about getting it, whether it is directed at you personally or your operation – or both. Remember it takes many forms: talking through what's happening as a way of making sense of it; checking out intended actions with a wider audience to see if you have missed anything; putting words to turbulent feelings; normal-ising new experiences with others in the same boat; taking breaks and holidays to refresh and get a fresh perspective.

- How you act will influence how others are towards you. Asking for the type of support *you* need in direct and open ways rather than through the back door allows others to deliver more of what you want.

Work the transition as a process not an event

- Transitions are not an event which begin and end with the "things" of position: a job contract, a share option, a desk, a team, an assistant. The model which holds that you are the "changer" who enters the organisation with a brief to "change it" whilst remaining unchanged yourself by the experience is one that hinders transition. Apart from its obvious difficulty – how can one person change a system as complex as an organisation anyway? It is not borne out by experience. When you see transition as a process, you see the organisation as fundamentally connected. You also realise that trying to change one part will impact every other. You do not believe in making change happen single-handedly. As your transition progresses and you behave differently, so does how the organisation reacts to you, which prompts new behaviour in you, which ... and so on.

- Most leaders like it best when "things are happening." They thrive on activity, which is why it is so reassuring to be faced with a heavy agenda. But an important part of any transition is sometimes to watch and listen to people with different ears and eyes. What you see and what you hear will be different at such times: you pick up subtler information, make yourself available to others differently and give yourself a better chance to digest your own experience. Leaders who thought of a new role as an event, were constantly shaken and surprised by the length of time they felt disorientated. Seeing it as a process of personal change lasting several months helps to make the temporary feelings of chaos and incompetence seem more normal. There is reassurance in being able to calibrate where you might be against the features of that stage of transition.

- The urgency to take immediate control of events, to stride in and act quickly was the main preference of our leaders. Only when they realised, as some did, that they would have to backtrack on plans as they got to better understand the context and the real nature of their mission, did the reality of working their transition as a process begin to land. This was often the moment when they began to appreciate what a systemic kind of leadership really involved and when they started to look more rigorously at themselves and how they were impacting their situation.

* * *

People often ask, how do you know when you reach the end of a transition? There is no definitive answer. But we have asked leaders this question and here's what they say, so we'll let them have the last word on the subject:

- You just know.

- You feel on top of things.

- When you've implemented something and had to manage the after-effects.

- You know who to ask and where to go to really get things done.

- When the same issues start coming round again.

- When all the faces around you have changed.

Bibliography

Gilles Amado and Richard Elsner, *Leaders et Transitions: Les dilemmes de la prise de poste* (Village Mondial, Paris, 2004).

Mary Catherine Bateson, *Composing a Life* (Grove Press, London, 1993).

George Binney, Gerhard Wilke, Colin Williams et al, *Leaders in Transition, The dramas of ordinary heroes* (Ashridge, Berkhamsted, 2003)

William Bridges, *Managing Transitions: Making the most of change* (Nicholas Brealey, London, 1991).

Dan Ciampa and Michael Watkins, *Right from the Start: Taking charge in a new leadership role* (Harvard Business School Press, Cambridge MA, 1999).

David L. Dotlich, James L. Noel and Norman Walker, *Leadership Passages: The personal and professional transitions that make or break a leader* (Jossey-Bass, San Francisco, 2004).

David L. Dotlich and Peter C. Cairo, *Why CEOs Fail: The 11 behaviors that can derail your climb to the top – and how to manage them* (Jossey-Bass, San Francisco, 2003).

John J. Gabarro, *The Dynamics of Taking Charge* (Harvard Business School Press, Cambridge MA, 1987).

Thomas N. Gilmore, *Making a leadership change: How organizations and leaders can handle leadership transitions successfully* (Jossey-Bass, San Francisco, 1988).

Barry Johnson, *Polarity Management: Identifying and managing unsolvable problems* (HRD Press, Amherst MA, 1992).

Dan P. McAdams, *The Stories We Live By: Personal myths and the making of the self* (Guilford Press, New York, 1993).

Morgan W. McCall, Jr and George P. Hollenbeck, *Developing Global Executives: The lessons of international experience* (Harvard Business School Press, Cambridge MA, 2002).

Morgan W. McCall, Jr, *High Flyers: Developing the next generation of leaders* (Harvard Business School Press, Cambridge MA, 1998).

Thomas J. Neff and James M. Citrin, *You're in Charge – Now What?: The 8-point plan* (Crown Business, New York, 2005).

Studs Terkel, *Working: People talk about what they do all day and how they feel about what they do* (The New Press, New York, 1997).

Eckhart Tolle, *A New Earth: Awakening to your life's purpose* (Michael Joseph, London, 2005).

M. A. Waller, "Resilience in ecosystemic context: Evolution of the concept," *American Journal of Orthopsychiatry*, 71 (3) 2001, pp. 332–58 cited in J. Melnick and S. M. Nevis, "Optimism: The willing suspension of belief," *Gestalt Review*, 9 (1) 2005, pp. 10–26.

Michael Watkins, *The First 90 Days: Critical success strategies for new leaders at all levels* (Harvard Business School Press, Cambridge MA, 2003).

Karl E. Weick, *Sensemaking in Organisations* (Sage Publications, London, 1995).

David Whyte, *The Heart Aroused: Poetry and the preservation of the soul in corporate America* (Currency, New York, 1996).

Appendix:
Personal Style Questionnaire

Instructions for completion

- Please read all of these instructions carefully before beginning.

- This questionnaire contains 96 statements. Please circle the one answer that best corresponds to your agreement or disagreement as shown below.

Circle "SD" if the statement is definitely false or if you **Strongly Disagree**.

(SD) D N A SA

Circle "D" if the statement is mostly false or if you **Disagree**.

SD (D) N A SA

Circle "N" if the statement is about equally true or false, if you cannot decide, or if you are **Neutral** on a statement.

SD D (N) A SA

Circle "A" if the statement is mostly true or if you **Agree**.

SD D N (A) SA

Circle "SA" if the statement is definitely true or if you **Strongly Agree**.

SD D N A (SA)

Advice on completing the questionnaire

- There are no right or wrong answers; the questionnaire is not assessing your intellectual ability.
- Try to describe yourself honestly and state your opinions openly.
- Do not spend too long on the questions. Initial impressions and spontaneous answers are best.
- Answer every question – if you are unsure, mark the response which comes closest to how you feel.
- If you make a mistake or change your mind, mark an X through the response you want to change and circle the one you wish to give.

---

1   I really enjoy change and variety.

   SD   D   N   A   SA

2   I like to work towards long-term goals.

   SD   D   N   A   SA

3   It is important to me that I am valued on the basis of my technical/professional competence.

   SD   D   N   A   SA

4   I really enjoy the opportunity to contribute my ideas.

   SD   D   N   A   SA

5   It is important to be to be firm and decisive.

   SD   D   N   A   SA

6   I am highly competitive and need to keep ahead.

   SD   D   N   A   SA

7   I am business focused and value competence in people.

   SD   D   N   A   SA

8   I tend to think and act in the interests of the organisation
    as a whole.

    SD   D   N   A   SA

9   I see myself as valuing tradition and stability.

    SD   D   N   A   SA

10 I think a clear direction emerges as a result of being attentive
    to your environment and becoming aware of what is needed.

    SD   D   N   A   SA

11 I really enjoy helping other people out.

    SD   D   N   A   SA

12 If I am not sure about something, I like to ask others and
    explore issues.

    SD   D   N   A   SA

13 I like to include people in decisions and ask them to contribute
    their ideas.

    SD   D   N   A   SA

14 I dislike taking decisions on little information.

    SD   D   N   A   SA

15 I think "people learn through their mistakes"; they should feel
    fully supported and encouraged to take risks.

    SD   D   N   A   SA

16 I really value teamwork above formal organisational goals.

    SD   D   N   A   SA

17 Life would be boring without change.

SD   D   N   A   SA

18 I like to work towards clear outcomes that I can name and describe.

SD   D   N   A   SA

19 I conduct relationships at work on a business-like basis and with a degree of formality.

SD   D   N   A   SA

20 If I go to a meeting, I expect to be able to actively and positively contribute rather than just attend.

SD   D   N   A   SA

21 Decisions should be taken and implemented quickly.

SD   D   N   A   SA

22 I have a lot of energy and like to keep busy.

SD   D   N   A   SA

23 I am prepared to be bold and radical in the way I implement change.

SD   D   N   A   SA

24 My primary duty is towards the business as a whole.

SD   D   N   A   SA

25 Traditional "tried and trusted" approaches to solving problems are usually best.

SD   D   N   A   SA

26 In order to achieve results you often need to adapt your goals to changing conditions.

SD   D   N   A   SA

27 It is really important to me that there is a climate of trust and openness where I work.

SD   D   N   A   SA

28 It is important to gather information and consult before introducing new initiatives.

SD   D   N   A   SA

29 It is important to get the support of staff before making decisions.

SD   D   N   A   SA

30 Good decisions require seeing things from many points of view.

SD   D   N   A   SA

31 It is really important that everyone is genuinely committed to their own and others' personal and longer-term development.

SD   D   N   A   SA

32 I am very loyal to my colleagues and value loyalty and collaboration over conflict.

SD   D   N   A   SA

33 I really enjoy the challenge of change.

SD   D   N   A   SA

34 I drive very hard towards gaols and am not easily distracted.

SD   D   N   A   SA

35 Generally I prefer to work on things on my own.

SD   D   N   A   SA

36 I like to find out what is happening in the organisation beyond my own area of work.

SD   D   N   A   SA

37 I have clear boundaries about what is negotiable and what isn't.

SD   D   N   A   SA

38 I enjoy working in a fast-paced energetic environment.

SD   D   N   A   SA

39 It is necessary to take the hard decisions to ensure performance is maintained/improved.

SD   D   N   A   SA

40 My duty is to support the organization's goals even if this is sometimes hard on my team.

SD   D   N   A   SA

41 I believe in the saying "If it isn't broken – don't fix it."

SD   D   N   A   SA

42 "Going with the flow" is often more effective than "sticking to your guns."

SD   D   N   A   SA

43 Personal relationships and the ability to get on with others are really important in my approach.

SD   D   N   A   SA

44 It is important to me to feel that I am really contributing in whatever I do.

SD   D   N   A   SA

45 I have a consultative style and like to reach decisions in cooperation with others.

SD   D   N   A   SA

46 I prepare really carefully before moving into execution on projects.

SD   D   N   A   SA

47 People do better if they feel valued for their efforts.

SD   D   N   A   SA

48 My primary loyalty is to my team.

SD   D   N   A   SA

49 I get frustrated if people or events get in the way of making changes.

SD   D   N   A   SA

50 I believe you create your own future by always having clear objectives to work to.

SD   D   N   A   SA

51 I find working closely with people for long tends to make me tired.

SD   D   N   A   SA

52 I feel confident in what I am saying when talking or contributing to decisions.

SD   D   N   A   SA

53 I think clarity of direction is more important than consultation.

SD   D   N   A   SA

54 I enjoy the pressure of having to deliver against tight time scales.

SD   D   N   A   SA

55 It is important to change/remove what/who is not working well.

SD   D   N   A   SA

56 The organization's goals are paramount and needs of individuals are always secondary.

SD   D   N   A   SA

57 Things that have lasted the test of time are good.

SD   D   N   A   SA

58 It is really important to respond to events as they happen, rather than being fixated on specific goals.

SD   D   N   A   SA

59 I really like to feel that I belong to a team.

SD   D   N   A   SA

60 I often ask for feedback or advice so I can improve what I do.

SD   D   N   A   SA

61 It is important to achieve a "consensus" before decisions are implemented.

SD   D   N   A   SA

62 I don't like being forced to reach decisions quickly and without adequate preparation.

SD   D   N   A   SA

63 I like to take a positive attitude and help promote a sense of personal growth and opportunity.

SD   D   N   A   SA

64 Managers have a primary duty to protect and nurture team members in a difficult organisational environment.

SD   D   N   A   SA

65 Change is definitely a positive thing.

SD   D   N   A   SA

66 In my life I have always been focused on future achievements.

SD   D   N   A   SA

67 I am a private person and keep my home and work lives clearly separate.

SD   D   N   A   SA

68 I really enjoy opportunities to teach and coach others by sharing my own knowledge and experience.

SD   D   N   A   SA

69 I believe that managers should take the decisions at work.

SD   D   N   A   SA

70 I really feel the need to get on with things.

SD   D   N   A   SA

71 It is sometimes necessary to "let people go."

SD   D   N   A   SA

72 The manager's role is to meet the organization's needs even where these conflict with the needs and preferences of the team.

SD   D   N   A   SA

73 I believe that stability and security are important at work.

SD   D   N   A   SA

74 I tend to respond very quickly to urgent matters as they arise whatever the original plan.

SD   D   N   A   SA

75 The ability to get on with others is the key to success.

SD   D   N   A   SA

76 It is important to have a good understanding of a subject before acting.

SD   D   N   A   SA

77 I have a democratic and inclusive approach.

SD   D   N   A   SA

78 I think things through carefully before reaching decisions.

SD   D   N   A   SA

79 I actively coach and help others if I can even if they are just a colleague.

SD   D   N   A   SA

80 I believe it is really important to support people so that they are
    prepared to "have a go."

    SD   D   N   A   SA

81 Things stagnate if we don't constantly challenge how we
    do things.

    SD   D   N   A   SA

82 I am uncomfortable when I do not have very clear
    objectives/goals to work towards.

    SD   D   N   A   SA

83 I don't like people who are over friendly or "touchy feely."

    SD   D   N   A   SA

84 I believe in proposing solutions not just in pointing out problems.

    SD   D   N   A   SA

85 I think clarity of direction is more important than consultation.

    SD   D   N   A   SA

86 The quicker you work the more you achieve.

    SD   D   N   A   SA

87 I enjoy working in a tough and demanding environment.

    SD   D   N   A   SA

88 The prime responsibility of a manager is to support the objectives
    of the organization, rather than pander to the wants and needs
    of individual team members.

    SD   D   N   A   SA

89 I am reluctant to try out new approaches unless they have been well demonstrated.

SD   D   N   A   SA

90 I have found that the most import thing is to adapt to the current situation rather than being too rigid about your goals.

SD   D   N   A   SA

91 Loyalty and respect between colleagues is a central value of mine.

SD   D   N   A   SA

92 I believe in the saying "Look, Listen, Learn."

SD   D   N   A   SA

93 If people are involved in decisions they take more responsibility for the outcomes.

SD   D   N   A   SA

94 I am often the one to suggest that we stand back and take time to think before we commit to action.

SD   D   N   A   SA

95 It gives me a real sense of satisfaction to see someone I have helped move on to better things.

SD   D   N   A   SA

96 Leaders should be expected to represent and defend their teams.

SD   D   N   A   SA

Instructions for completing your profile

Now transfer your answers to the table opposite and give yourself a score for each answer as follows:

If you answered **Strongly Disagree** you get a score of **0**

If you answered **Disagree** you get a score of **1**

If you answered **Neutral** you get a score of **2**

If you answered **Agree** you get a score of **3**

If you answered **Strongly Agree** you get a score of **4**

Write each of your scores next to the question numbers. Work your way down the column, skipping a row each time then come back to the top. Continue with the next column and so on.

When you have completed all the scoring, add up your score in each row and put the total for that row in the shaded box on the right-hand side. (You will see each row is headed by the name of one of the Preferences. So row 1 is headed "Shake up," row 2 "Preserve," row 3 "Intentional" etc.)

Question numbers and scores   Totals

MISSION
Shake up   1 ___   17 ___ 33 ___ 49 ___ 65 ___ 81 ___

Preserve   9 ___   25 ___ 41 ___ 57 ___ 73 ___ 89 ___

GOAL ORIENTATION
Intentional   2 ___   18 ___ 34 ___ 50 ___ 66 ___ 82 ___

Emergent   10 ___ 26 ___ 42 ___ 58 ___ 74 ___ 90 ___

RELATIONSHIPS
Keep distance   3 ___   19 ___ 35 ___ 51 ___ 67 ___ 83 ___

Develop bonds   11 ___ 27 ___ 43 ___ 59 ___ 75 ___ 91 ___

RECIPROCITY
Give value   4 ___   20 ___ 36 ___ 52 ___ 68 ___ 84 ___

Seek help   12 ___ 28 ___ 44 ___ 60 ___ 76 ___ 92 ___

DECISION MAKING
Impose   5 ___   21 ___ 37 ___ 53 ___ 69 ___ 85 ___

Facilitate   13 ___ 29 ___ 45 ___ 61 ___ 77 ___ 93 ___

PACE OF CHANGE
Go fast   6 ___   22 ___ 38 ___ 54 ___ 70 ___ 86 ___

Go slow   14 ___ 30 ___ 46 ___ 62 ___ 78 ___ 94 ___

FAITH
Clean out   7 ___   23 ___ 39 ___ 55 ___ 71 ___ 87 ___

Develop   15 ___ 31 ___ 47 ___ 63 ___ 79 ___ 95 ___

LOYALTY
Serve the hierarchy 8 ___ 24 ___ 40 ___ 56 ___ 72 ___ 88 ___

Support the team 16 ___ 32 ___ 48 ___ 64 ___ 80 ___ 96 ___

Creating your chart

Now transfer your scores to the chart below. You do this by looking at your total score in the shaded box for each Pole then drawing a line away from the centre to the number that matches your score for that Pole. So, as an example if you scored 20 for "Shake up," you would draw a thick line (we suggest you use a felt tip pen) from the centre of the chart over to the side towards "Shake up" and stop at the number 20.

	Preference		
	Strong	Moderate	Weak

MISSION
Shake up　　24 22 20 18 16 14 12 10 8 6 4 2 0

GOAL ORIENTATION
Intentional　　24 22 20 18 16 14 12 10 8 6 4 2 0

RELATIONSHIPS
Keep distance　　24 22 20 18 16 14 12 10 8 6 4 2 0

RECIPROCITY
Give value　　24 22 20 18 16 14 12 10 8 6 4 2 0

DECISION MAKING
Impose　　24 22 20 18 16 14 12 10 8 6 4 2 0

PACE OF CHANGE
Go fast　　24 22 20 18 16 14 12 10 8 6 4 2 0

FAITH
Clean out　　24 22 20 18 16 14 12 10 8 6 4 2 0

LOYALTY
Serve the hierarchy　　24 22 20 18 16 14 12 10 8 6 4 2 0

Key: **BOLD** = TENSION; *Italics* = Pole

Now do this for your own score stopping at the number you actually got for "Shake up." Then repeat the process for "Preserve" this time drawing your line across to the right towards the words "Preserve." For example, if you scored 10 then you would draw a line across to the 10. Now do this for your own score stopping at the number you actually got for "Preserve."

Preference

Weak		Moderate	Strong	

0 2 4 6 8 10 12 14 16 18 20 22 24	*Preserve*
0 2 4 6 8 10 12 14 16 18 20 22 24	*Emergent*
0 2 4 6 8 10 12 14 16 18 20 22 24	*Develop bonds*
0 2 4 6 8 10 12 14 16 18 20 22 24	*Seek help*
0 2 4 6 8 10 12 14 16 18 20 22 24	*Facilitate*
0 2 4 6 8 10 12 14 16 18 20 22 24	*Go slow*
0 2 4 6 8 10 12 14 16 18 20 22 24	*Develop*
0 2 4 6 8 10 12 14 16 18 20 22 24	*Support the team*

Interpreting your chart

If you now look down the chart, what do you observe?

Within each tension

The length of the line for each pole tells you how strong your tendency is to act in this way. Look at the lines for the poles of each tension, and identify which ones have "weak," "moderate" and "strong" intensity. What do you see?

If a line represents a moderate score, you are naturally disposed to act in this way, and have developed considerable familiarity with the behaviour in question. You will also find it relatively easy to develop new ways of exhibiting this behaviour. Others will see you as being "at home" and skilled in this way of acting. If a line represents a strong score, you have an unusual and pronounced tendency to act in this way. You will almost certainly recognise your marked preference to act in this way, and will probably find it difficult to move flexibly to the other pole. You will probably be seen by others to be exceptional, even possibly extreme, in this behaviour. Finally, if a line represents a weak score, you have a reduced tendency to act in this way, and may even perceive yourself as having a blind-spot in this regard. Others may see you as less developed, even possibly weak, in this regard.

Within each tension, examine the relationship between the two poles. Let us look at the most frequent cases.

It is likely that with some of the tensions one pole will be significantly more developed than the other. If that is the case, you have a "preference" for that pole. If, for example, one pole is either moderate or even strong, and the other weak, then you have a preference for one side of the tension. To have a preference means that you will lean naturally to exhibiting the behaviour of that pole, which will be like your "suit." You will be probably feel less comfortable exhibiting the behaviour associated with the other pole. That pole will feel somewhat foreign, and you may feel unsighted or awkward when trying our behaviours associated with it.

With other tensions, you may find that the poles have broadly equal scores (within 2–3 points). When that happens, you have broadly equal fluency with the behaviours of both poles. This will result in your appearing balanced to your colleagues. It will also probably be the case that you can switch with relative ease between the two poles, because of their equivalent intensity. The ability to switch between poles will be a measure of the flexibility which you exhibit in managing the tension in question. In some cases the intensity of both poles will be weak, in which case you will not have particular breadth in respect of that tension. In other cases, the intensity of both poles will be moderate, in which case your breadth in the tension will be quite adequate to sustain you through a range of different situations. It is rarer for a leader to have strong intensity in both poles – when it happens it means that they are unusually broad and capable in the management of this tension.

Across the 8 Tensions

It is also helpful to look at what the aggregate of your preferences is across the 8 Tensions.

If you look again at the chart, you will note that the poles on the left hand represent task- and performance-focus, whereas the poles on the right hand represent a focus more on human and social concerns. Do your preferences lean more towards one side or the other?

If you have more than five preferences to the left, you can deduce that you have a natural predisposition towards performance and delivery of results, and will most likely subsume other concerns to their achievement. You will probably be seen as goal-driven and tough, and will have acquired a reputation for establishing high expectations of yourself and others.

If you have more than five preferences to the right, you can deduce that you have a natural predisposition towards developing and maintaining the strength of your organisation. You will be noted for your tendency to seek agreement and for the development of solutions which have wide ownership. You may be seen as particularly good with people, and concerned for their motivation.

If you have an equal number of preferences to the left and to the right, you will most likely be seen as balanced in your leadership behaviour, which depending on the context, can be helpful or otherwise. A lot depends on the intensity of the scores you have. If the intensity of the scores on the preferred poles is strong, you will probably stand out as original and free-thinking, but there is a risk that you may be perceived as difficult to predict, in that you may present a complex image as a leader. If the intensity of the scores on the preferred poles is mainly weak or moderate, you may well be seen as open-minded and accommodating, but there is a risk that you may be perceived as low profile or difficult to read.